The Yogic Manager

At the turning point between crisis and consciousness, one manager builds

A Bridge Between Yoga-Vedanta and Management

AVINASH B. SHARMA, MBA

Foreword by
DR. DIPAK C. JAIN, DEAN, INSEAD

The author can be reached at:
www.yogicmanagement.com

ISBN-13: 978-1482053036
ISBN-10: 1482053039

Dedicated to all of the past, present, and future
teachers, students, and practitioners of
Yoga, Vedanta and Management

We are facing a tremendous **crisis**; a crisis which the politicians can never solve because they are programmed to think in a particular way—nor can the scientists understand or solve the crisis; nor yet the business world, the world of money. The **turning point**, the perceptive decision, the challenge, is not in politics, in religion, in the scientific world, it is in our **consciousness**. One has to understand the consciousness of mankind, which has brought us to this point.
—Jiddu Krishnamurti

Contents

Foreword

Seeking a new global balance through reflection, renewal and responsibility

Global markets are extraordinary, powerful but also volatile. Capable of creating great value, they also can destroy that value quickly. We only need to reflect on the most recent financial crisis for proof of this Shiva-like dual role of business forces.

Economically and culturally, globalization has lifted millions out of poverty, providing hope and material comfort, while bringing us closer together in the marketplace. There, we create and share value, along with our traditions, ideas and experiences. In other words, through our material transactions we also share our *values and our humanity.*

But this same force, by integrating the world's markets as it has done, also increases complexity, connectivity, and competitiveness while raising the stakes higher than they have ever been. If we are all connected, then errors in managerial judgment in one part of the world will ripple out to impact other parts of the system—as we saw with the 2008 banking meltdown, whose affects are still lingering. Similarly, decisions by those who manage organizations—especially vast, multinational enterprises—will impact many people and human behavior and our natural environment.

Each of us, then, has a vested interest in cultivating more *holistic* managers whose actions are guided by a balanced framework, such as the one Avinash Sharma offers in this book. By drawing from ancient Vedantic wisdom, he seeks to provide modern managers with a robust, aspirational model that can help them and their organizations play a transformative part in making the world a better and safer place.

Simply pursuing process optimizations or repeating Gordon Gekko's mantra "Greed is good" will not do. The framework of profit maximization and market "efficiencies" to the exclusion of all else may lead to an unsustainable path. The evidence is all around us, in the air and water and landfills and in serious economic disparities that can fuel division among people. Profit is fine, of course, and acts as a useful incentive. Efficiency is fine too, but it is a curious metric, since one can be efficient without being wise or even especially thoughtful. In fact, these considerations must be balanced with other considerations, including the well being of all stakeholders, not just shareholders.

The Yogic Manager does not ask executives to join an ashram, or cast aside their pinstripe suits in favor of a sadhu's robe. In a way, that course of action might be easier. More challenging is remaining at the heart of the commercial world while balancing the discipline and values of *dharma* with the material practices of *artha* and worldly pleasures of *kama*. Achieving this balance leads to what I call *purpose with performance*—a meaningful life whose riches enrich and whose achievements bless oneself and others.

I started my educational journey with advice from my parents to learn the classic "3 R's"—*reading, (w)riting* and *(a)rithmetic*. Our professional journey depends also on what I consider the new 3 R's, or *reflection, renewal* and *responsibility*. Managers, like all of us, can cultivate *mindfulness* that leads to self-knowledge and an understanding of how our thoughts, words and actions create karmic results. These insights offer a chance for us to *renew* both strategy and spirit. This journey into Self is incomplete without returning back into the world with a fuller sense of one's *responsibility* to others and to the world. After all, the soul of management is about nurturing and challenging others to be their best. It is about relationships. It is about *people, process* and *purpose*.

In business we speak of best practices—methods that prove useful again and again. In science, we talk of empirical evidence, derived from data that comes from multiple experiments. When such evidence is produced repeatedly, we establish a scientific law. Yoga has been with us since antiquity, with countless generations celebrating its benefits. Now, it has the potential to provide managers with insight, inspiration and integrity of body, mind and spirit to enable them to achieve their quarterly results and much, much more.

This book provides us with a path from knowledge to wisdom.

Dr. Dipak C. Jain
Dean, INSEAD

Introduction

We build too many walls and not enough bridges.
—Isaac Newton

Purpose of this Book

The book that you are reading was written to be more than a business novel and self-improvement guide. It was written to be a bridge.

On one end of this bridge lies the multidisciplinary practice of Management, which evolved by incorporating ideas from a variety of other fields—economics, psychology, sociology, the military, neuroscience, and more.

On the other end of this bridge lies the practice of Yoga and the philosophies of Vedanta. The ancient Sanskrit scriptures, such as the Upanishads and the Bhagavad Gita, provide a blueprint for living a balanced and purposeful life. I will refer to the union of practice (Yoga) and theory (Vedanta) as Yoga-Vedanta.

Are there concepts from Yoga-Vedanta that managers can apply to make themselves better managers? Can Management incorporate teachings from Yoga-Vedanta in the same way it incorporates teachings from other fields? In the process, can managers gain fulfillment from their work, become more holistic in their thinking, and contribute toward the betterment of society and the environment? My research, education, and experience in these subjects indicate that the answer to all these questions is "yes." I will refer to this union of Management and Yoga-Vedanta as **Yogic Management**.

Defining Yoga

Yoga, for the purpose of this book, is defined by the following two verses from the Bhagavad Gita:

Being steadfast in Yoga, Dhananjaya [Prince Arjuna], perform actions, abandoning attachment, remaining unconcerned as regards success and failure. This *samatvam* [evenness, balance] of mind (in regard to success and failure) is known as Yoga. [2.48]
Endued with this evenness of mind, one frees oneself in this life, alike

3

from vice and virtue. Devote thyself, therefore, to this Yoga. Yoga is the very *kausalam* [art, skill] of work. [2.50]
—Lord Krishna in the Bhagavad Gita, 2.48 and 2.50

In these verses, there are two definitions of Yoga. The first is in *samatvam*, verse 2.48: **Yoga is evenness or balance of mind**. The second is in *kausalam*, verse 2.50: **Yoga is the art of work** or skill in action.

Defining Management

Management has been described in many different ways ever since people started studying it as a discipline. The following is a description by Peter Drucker, who has greatly influenced my thinking:

> Management, in most business schools, is still taught as a bundle of techniques, such as the technique of budgeting. To be sure, management, like any other work, has its own tools and its own techniques. But just as the essence of medicine is not the urinalysis, important though it is, the essence of management is not techniques and procedures. **The essence of management is to make knowledge productive.**
> —Peter Drucker[1]

This description is very relevant to the current age, which is often referred to as the Knowledge Age, an age in which knowledge is a key resource. The period before this was referred to as the Industrial Age, an age in which work was done primarily with the human hand and the operation of machines. **In the Industrial Age, the instrument of manual work was the human hand. In the Knowledge Age, the instrument of knowledge work is the human mind.**

Productivity gains in our modern knowledge economy are dependent not upon machines and the human body, but upon the human mind. The mind is more subtle than physical objects and is more difficult to study. However, scholars of Yoga-Vedanta have studied the mind for several thousand years and have developed philosophies and practices that address how the mind can be matured and made more productive.

The etymology of the English word "manage" is from the Old French word *'manège'* ("the handling or training of a horse"). The French word has its roots in the Italian *'maneggiare'* ("to handle"), which comes from the Latin *'manus'* ("the hand").[2] It follows that Management is associated with the hand, a connection that was appropriate in the Industrial Age when most work was done manually.

In Sanskrit, the word for "mind" is *'manas'*; in modern South Asian

4

languages, it is 'man' (pronounced "muhn," as in "human"). In this book, I propose a new definition of Management that is better suited to the Knowledge Age.

"Management" is 'man' (mind) plus 'agement' (making mature). Management is the act of making knowledge productive by maturing the instruments of knowledge work—the minds of the people involved in the work.

Synopsis

This book is a business novel and a modern retelling of the ancient Sanskrit epic, the Mahabharata. The epic's war of Kurukshetra has been recreated in the world of business at a consulting firm called Characterra Consulting. The protagonist is Arjun Atmanand who faces a crisis when his conscience clashes with the instructions of his boss and Characterra's founder, Raja Sahamkar. To help him with his crisis, Arjun receives advice from Yogi, a being with supernatural powers. Arjun learns Yoga and Vedanta from Yogi, which he uses to build a bridge between Yoga-Vedanta and Management.

Arjun develops a set of Yogic Management frameworks and principles that are the foundations of this bridge:
1. Reality-Consciousness-Bliss Framework
2. Knowledge Work Equation
3. Motive-Mind-Means Framework
4. Purposeful Life Framework
5. Principles of Yogic Management
6. Yogic Management Mantra

These frameworks and principles were inspired by the following Yoga-Vedanta concepts:
1. Four Values of Life (*Purusharthas*)
2. Five Sheaths of the Human Body (*Pancha Koshas*)
3. Four Phases/Houses of Life (*Ashrams*)
4. Five Elements (*Pancha Bhutas*)
5. Seven Energy Centers/Wheels (*Chakras*)

This book quotes from the Mahabharata, Bhagavad Gita, Upanishads, and Yoga Sutras.[3] The Sanskrit words are presented in italics.

For a longer discussion of the connections between characters and events in the Mahabharata and in *The Yogic Manager*, see the epilogue.

What You Will Gain From This Book

By reading and studying this book, you will:
—Start to challenge conventional ways of thinking about business and gain a new, holistic perspective of Management;
—Learn the principles and frameworks of Yogic Management, which you can then apply immediately to your work;
—Become a more productive knowledge worker by learning how to control and channel the power of the instrument of knowledge work, your mind;
—Gain fulfillment through your work and, in the process, contribute toward the betterment of society and all life on Earth;
—Gain practical advice on how to build physical, mental, intellectual, and spiritual strength;
—Live a balanced and purposeful life by going through the four phases prescribed in Yoga-Vedanta; and
—Join, should you wish to, the evolution of Management, a movement that will elevate the human condition and restore harmony to an imbalanced planet

The frameworks (as high resolution charts in full color) and other resources have been made available for free on the website.
www.yogicmanagement.com

Avinash Bhushan Sharma, MBA
Toronto, Canada
January 2013

1. Dreams and Memories

Eight years ago, my life changed forever. The events from that day still flash into my mind with such clarity that they feel like they happened just minutes ago.

I was a twenty-one-year-old student and was about to take the biggest step of my life.

I remember standing with countless other people outside the United States Embassy in New Delhi. In my hand was a file with a variety of documents needed to obtain the F-1 Student Visa. Amongst these documents was the Form I-20. This showed that I, Arjun Atmanand, had been accepted by the University of Chicago into the Master of Science in Financial Mathematics program.

Everything should have gone smoothly. My brother Karan had successfully gone through the same process two years ago. He had helped me get my paperwork together and I knew that all my documents were in order. The September 11th terrorist attacks on the United States were still fresh in peoples' memories. Student visas could be denied for the slightest of reasons. However, I wasn't worried. The University of Chicago was eager to bring me in. I had completed the Graduate Record Examination (GRE) with a high overall score, including a perfect score, 800 out of 800, in the quantitative section. I had the document showing my GRE results with me. Karan had insisted that I be extremely thorough in my application process.

Everything should have gone smoothly—but it didn't.

When it was my turn, I was ushered to the glass window separating me from the interviewer. A stern American woman, who seemed bored with the monotony of her job, sifted through my application. It was almost the end of the day and I could tell she was ready to call it a night. I hoped she would be quick.

It started well. Her questions were straightforward and my answers were to the point.

And then the most bizarre of events occurred. Even though the windows in the room were covered with curtains, a light started to form to my right. I stopped looking at the woman and stared at this light, which I can best describe as having a soft golden color. It was not as powerful as staring directly at the sun, which one cannot do for more than a few fractions of a second. Yet it felt a bit like sunlight—warm and inviting. It started as a circle and then began to turn into the form of a human being sitting in the cross-legged lotus pose, or *padmasana*. Although I could not see the face, I could see that the being was a male yogi with a clean-shaven head. He was clothed below the waist, and wore a rosary and a few bracelets made of seeds. He stayed for about ten seconds before shrinking back down to a circle and disappearing completely.

The interviewer repeated a question a few times while I was lost in the light, but I didn't hear what it was. By the time my attention returned to her, it was too late. She was irritated and told me my visa was denied. I left the embassy in a state of shock. I hardly knew what had hit me.

"Arjun. Arjun."

A woman's voice broke through my thoughts, but this time it had an Indian accent. I forced my mind to return to the present. As my eyes began to focus on the room, I saw a diploma framed on the wall in front of me. It said Jyoti Ramasethu, Master of Science in Psychology. I then shifted my attention to Jyoti, who was sitting in a chair opposite me, with a tablet in one hand and a stylus pen in another.

'What am I doing here?' I thought. Then I remembered that this was Karan's mischief. He had flown in from New York a month ago on a business trip that spanned five major cities in India. When he met me here in Gurgaon, he used emotional blackmail to make me speak with a counselor. For some strange reason he believed that I was under a lot of stress and that I needed to speak with a professional to solve my problems. I don't know what problems he thinks I have. There is absolutely nothing wrong with me.

On the bright side, Jyoti was definitely someone I could enjoy spending time with. She was a tall, slender woman with a dusky complexion and wavy hair that she tried to tame by tying it up in a bun. Her large brown eyes darted intelligently behind her black-framed glasses and she had a pleasant and reassuring smile. I did some quick calculations based on the dates on her degree certificate. I estimated that she was around twenty-seven years old—rather young, I thought, to be advising people. But she happened to be highly recommended by Karan, who always did thorough research. It was a pity that I was meeting her under such awkward circumstances rather than over a cup of coffee.

"Arjun," she said again.

"Yes?"

"We were discussing your sleeping habits. We determined that sometimes you wake up really early in the morning and cannot go back to sleep. I asked you if you have any recurring dreams. And then you seemed to go into, well, deep thought. Were you remembering a dream?"

"It was not a dream," I said. "It was a memory of an event that occurred eight years ago."

"Do you get this memory during your sleep? And does it wake you up at night?"

"Yes."

"Then it's a dream as well as a memory. Please tell me about it."

I explained the dream to her, including the part about the strange golden light.

"And then the woman says, 'Your visa is denied.' That's when I wake up."

"This light—do you think it was a figment of your imagination?" Jyoti asked.

"No, it was not. I am a man of science. I do not believe in spirits or ghosts. I have said since I was a child that, 'If I can't see it, I won't believe it.' But that day I saw something. I don't know what it was, but it was there. I just can't understand why it had to reveal itself at that very moment, a turning point that would have forever changed my life."

Jyoti made some notes in her tablet.

"Do you get any other recurring dreams?" she asked.

I paused for a second or two. Something had come into my mind, but I was reluctant to talk about it.

"Go ahead," she said. "What were you thinking about?"

"Jyoti, I'm going to be frank with you. I really don't see the point of this exercise. I'm a normal guy—physically and mentally healthy. Sure, I have some stress every now and then. But, in today's world, who doesn't? I came here only because I was tricked by my brother, Karan. I don't need any counseling."

"Karan had called me a few weeks ago from New York," Jyoti said, with a smile. "He sure is persuasive—very difficult to say no to. He warned me that you would have your reservations about meeting me. Anyway, he has paid for ten sessions in advance. Now that we are here, how about we make the best of the situation and continue with this 'exercise?'"

I paused for a few seconds, sighed, and then smiled back at Jyoti.

"I have another recurring dream," I said. "This one is not a memory."

"Go ahead," said Jyoti, ready to scribble more notes into her tablet.

"I am running down a road. The road is made not of tar or concrete, but of reddish-brown earth. There are no turns on this road. You can either go forward or backward. Many people from my life are running with me on this road. My boss, Raja, is running, as are many of my colleagues from work. There are also some of my classmates from school and college, and a few of my cousins and other relatives. And running besides me is Karan. Sometimes Karan is a few feet ahead of me. Sometimes I am ahead by a few feet. But mostly we are running side by side. All of us are dressed in red[4] —red clothes, shoes, caps, and other accessories."

"Does the color red mean anything to you?" asked Jyoti.

"No," I replied, before proceeding with my narration. "After running for a while I start to recognize some of the spots we have run past. It dawns on me that we are running around in circles. I look up and see that the finishing point, marked by a red banner, is on top of a nearby hill. But the road does not lead to the finishing point. I slow down and stop. Karan also stops.

"'Don't stop,' Karan says to me. 'Continue running.'

"'We are running around in circles,' I say. 'This feels like the *Chakravyuh*.'"

"*Chakravyuh*?" interrupted Jyoti. "Are you referring to the battle formation from the war in the Mahabharata epic?"

"Yes," I replied. "It was an intricate, wheel-shaped battle formation. Of the warriors participating in the Great War, only Lord Krishna and Prince Arjuna could enter as well as exit the *Chakravyuh*."[5]

"Please continue," said Jyoti as she scribbled her notes.

I continued relating my dream.

"I ask Karan why I should keep running.

"'Because it is a race,' he replies. 'In order to win, you must run. If you quit, you will lose. If you are tired, take a little rest and then continue running.'

"'I'm not tired,' I tell him, 'but I don't see the point of running farther.'

"Karan says, 'You do as you wish. I'm going ahead,' and he starts running again. I watch him disappear into the crowd. Then I wake up."

"We may be onto something here," said Jyoti. "When did you start getting these recurring dreams?"

"They started around two years ago," I said.

"How frequently do you have these dreams?"

"At first, they were about once a month. Lately, they have been once or twice a week."

"What could have happened around two years ago to trigger your dreams and poor sleeping habits?"

"I can't think of any major event."

"Can you think of anything else that was common in your dreams?"

"Yes. For some strange reason, I always wake up at 4:42 a.m."

"Always at 4:42 a.m.?" Jyoti asked, surprised.

"Yes. The first thing I look at when I wake up is my alarm clock. And when I have these dreams, I always wake up at 4:42 a.m."

"Do the numbers 4 and 42 mean anything to you?"

"No."

Jyoti made a few more notes before she continued with her questions.

"Tell me more about the race. Did Karan and you compete a lot as children?" She asked.

"Not exactly. We have always been very similar. Whatever Karan

10

achieved, a couple of years later, I would achieve the same thing."

"Can you give me some specifics?" asked Jyoti.

"In middle school and high school he always scored the highest grades in his batch in mathematics. I did the same in my batch. In fact, we both scored the highest possible grade—a supposedly impossible feat. He was the chess champion in school. After he graduated, I also became the chess champion. In high school, Karan was selected to represent India at the International Mathematical Olympiad. He went on to win a gold medal. Two years later, I, too, represented India at the Olympiad, the most prestigious mathematical competition, and won a gold medal. To date, it is my most prized possession."

"Did the competition continue beyond high school?" asked Jyoti.

"After school, Karan went on to study at one of India's best universities. Two years later, I, too, went to study at the same university. Later, Karan received admission into the University of Chicago's Master of Science in Financial Mathematics program. This is a highly regarded niche program that specializes in the application of mathematics to finance, with a focus on derivatives."

At this point, Jyoti gave me a look of confusion.

"Derivatives," I continued "are financial products built using extremely complicated mathematical formulas. I also got admission into the University of Chicago for the same program. Karan got his visa to study in the United States. He went on to complete his studies and then moved to New York City to be an investment banker on Wall Street. He quickly rose through the ranks and within three years he was running a hedge fund. He is very skilled at reading the market. He saw the housing bubble coming and he bet against the market before it popped. Today his net worth is in the tens of millions of dollars. However, I did not get my student visa. After that point, I could not equal any of his achievements."

"What did you do instead of studying abroad?" asked Jyoti.

"I interviewed for jobs and found one with Characterra Consulting, where I have been working for the past eight years."

"What do you do at this firm?"

"I'm a management consultant. I advise our clients on their investment decisions. My specialty lies in building business cases, backed by financial models. I demonstrate the potential financial returns from different investment scenarios. In short, I advise clients on where to deploy their money to get the best return on investment."

"Is your work stressful?"

"At times it can get stressful. When you are dealing with financials you have got to be very careful. A tiny error in the formulas, even something as rudimentary as adding the wrong two cells, can lead someone to providing a client with the wrong advice. Often large sums of money are at stake."

"How many hours a week do you work?"

"I work long hours."

"How many?"

"I'm not sure. Maybe seventy hours a week."

"Does everyone at your firm work these hours?"

"No. I work the longest hours."

"Why do you work so much?"

At this point I paused for a few seconds. Nobody had asked me such questions before and I had never spent much time thinking about these issues.

"I guess it's because work helps me to focus my mind on something productive," I said. "Work makes me feel valued—as though the fact that I am alive and on this Earth matters to someone or the other. In the process, I am making money and being successful."

"Would you consider yourself to be a workaholic?" asked Jyoti.

"I wouldn't put labels on myself. And frankly, even if I were a workaholic, I don't see what the big deal is. I'm not addicted to cigarettes, alcohol, or drugs. I'm in good health and nobody is being harmed."

"Oftentimes, lifestyles that are out of balance do have health impacts—sometimes physical, sometimes psychological, sometimes both. Anyway, we are nearly done with our session today. Before we finish, I want to mention that I'm sensing an issue related to you not getting your visa to study in the United States. Your *Chakravyuh* dream indicates that you think that Karan, equal to you in every way, moved ahead and became very successful while you did not. Though in reality, it seems that you have been successful on your own. It's just that you have not been able to let go of the past and you keep thinking about 'what if' scenarios. It was not always like this. But something happened two years ago to trigger these emotions and related dreams. Before our next session, please put some thought into what could have happened two years ago."

"Sure," I said. "May I ask you a question?"

"Go ahead."

"I am an ordinary guy living an ordinary life, just like billions of other ordinary people living on Earth. I'm curious to know why you do this work. I mean, don't you find it boring and painful to listen to the mundane problems in the lives of ordinary people?"

Jyoti paused a few seconds before answering. She seemed to be surprised by the question.

"It is my belief that no life is ordinary," replied Jyoti. "If you look a little deeper into a person, just below the surface, you will realize that there are always some things that make her or him special. Some unique experience, some rare problem they have faced and maybe overcome, some uncommon talent, or some characteristic that makes them different from everyone else.

People have interesting stories worth hearing. I do this work because I like to hear those stories. How about we book our next session for the same time next week?"

"Next week may not be possible," I said. "How about I call you and schedule the next session?"

Jyoti gave me a suspicious look.

"Alright," she said. "You call me. But note that Karan has already paid for ten sessions and that I will not be calling you to schedule your next one."

"Sounds good," I replied. "It was a pleasure meeting you."

2. The Art of War

I went to work early the next day to attend a 5:00 a.m. meeting, via web conference, with a colleague in Brazil. As I punched in the security code to get into the Characterra Consulting premises, I could not help noticing the large map of the world hanging behind the receptionist's desk. Characterra's five global offices—New York City, Sao Paulo, Gurgaon, Jakarta, and Shanghai—were proudly highlighted. Although the firm had been in business for only eight years, it had grown exponentially.

I had been with the firm from the very beginning. As I walked to my office past the cubicles through the dark and desolate floor, I remembered the interview that got me hired at Characterra eight years ago. That was the day I first met Raja Sahamkar, one of the five founders of Characterra Consulting and the managing partner of Characterra India. Raja had just moved from New York to Gurgaon to set up the office and get a share of one of the world's fastest-growing economies. All five founders were graduates of the same MBA cohort at a highly ranked business school. They had all gone on to gain experience at the world's leading management consulting firms and then, some years later, they had decided to set up their own firm, with offices in each of their home countries. The founders, as well as the employees, collaborated closely with their colleagues from all five offices.

I remembered the interview as if it happened yesterday. I had just graduated and was searching for a job. Raja was looking for someone with a strong quantitative background who he could train to do financials and analytics in the manner in which he wanted to do them. My gold medal at the Mathematical Olympiad had superseded the fact that I had no work experience.

Raja was thirty-three years old then. I remember him as being stern, self-confident, and extremely passionate about his new venture. He wore a perfectly fitted black suit with a white shirt and a red tie. He was also wearing a Rolex watch and an interesting pair of cufflinks designed as two playing cards. It showed the letters "K" and "A", for the King of Hearts and Ace of Spades. On a later occasion, Raja explained their significance.

"'K' + 'A' = 21," Raja had said to me. "It is the winning score in blackjack. It also means that I am a king and always have an ace up my sleeve."

In addition to his attire, the first thing I noticed about Raja was his

American accent, gained from fifteen years of education and work experience in the United States. Raja liked to say that people took him more seriously because of his accent and that this allowed him to charge our clients a 20% premium on fees.

The interview felt less like an interview and more like an interrogation. To many of my answers, Raja would ask additional questions to drill deeper into the answers I had provided. Twenty minutes into the interview I began to feel that things were not going my way. Raja was talking to me with a tone of arrogance and superiority, and he looked bored with my answers. "What is your greatest strength?" asked Raja.

"I am skilled in converting data into information and then applying the information as knowledge," I replied. "If you give me data, I will process it to give you information. If you give me information, I will apply it as knowledge to give you results."

In many interviews, there comes a turning point—a question and answer that define the outcome of the interview. This interview's turning point came in the form of the following question.

"Then, what is wisdom?" asked Raja.

"I don't know what wisdom is." I stopped trying to respond calmly and politely. "To me it's one of the many buzzwords concocted by business gurus that is fancy sounding but lacking in substance."

Perhaps it was Raja's attitude that prompted me to speak like he was speaking to me. Raja paused for a couple of seconds and then smiled. He leaned back on his chair comfortably and laughed.

"Guess what?" he said. "I also don't know what wisdom is. I think you are a horse I'd be willing to bet some money on."

He offered me the job immediately after that. I was Characterra's employee number ten, including the five global partners. The salary and other benefits were greater than I expected. After accepting the job, I began growing along with the firm. I started as an analyst when we had only six people in the Indian office. In two years, I was promoted to senior consultant. Four years after that, I was promoted to principal consultant and was given my own office—a luxury that made many of my older colleagues jealous. Today, Characterra has around two hundred employees globally, one hundred of whom are located in India. The five partners were followed in rank by a dozen principal consultants, including me.

Much of the exponential growth could be attributed to Raja's passion for Characterra. In addition to passion, he had intelligence and came from a very wealthy family that used to be royalty. His grandfather was the last in his family to hold the title of "Raja" (king). The family had an arrangement with the British Empire. Although under British rule, they got to function as a princely state and retain their properties. Sometime after India gained independence from British rule, Raja's family used their wealth to invest in a variety of companies and real estate ventures that turned out to be very profitable over the years. Some of his relatives used their royal heritage to become high-ranking politicians, an extremely lucrative career given the rampant corruption. Though he was the heir to the throne, Raja did not inherit any kingdom or title. But his grandfather named him such that he would still be "Raja Sahamkar."

When Characterra was launched, he brought in most of the seed funding. He owned 60% of the firm while the other four partners owned 10% each. With this setup, even if the other four partners voted together, they could not veto any of Raja's decisions. Hence he got to be the King of Characterra and did things exactly the way he wanted, and he knew exactly what he wanted.

A meeting at 5:00 a.m. is never easy. Especially if the person you are meeting is located on the other side of the world. Armed with strong coffee from the espresso machine in the Characterra kitchen, I attended the web conference with Silvia Costa, a senior consultant from the Sao Paulo office. Over the last two months, I had been providing the analytics for a large business case in the oil and gas industry. Our meetings had been for two or three hours, three times a week. This was our last meeting, where we were reviewing the final presentation prepared for our clients. I was happy with this presentation. There were tables, charts, and graphs in multiple colors, with numbers and explanations that business executives would want to see and hear. In the world of business, this kind of presentation would be called "a work of art." Though the engagement was challenging and had high visibility with the partners, I was glad it was coming to an end. The early hours were making worse my already irregular sleeping habits.

Silvia had joined Characterra Consulting in Sao Paulo around two years ago after completing her MBA at a top American school. While we spent most of our meetings building presentations, documents, and complex spreadsheets, every now and then she would ask about India and Indian culture. Apparently, there was a popular Brazilian television soap opera based on India.

After my meeting I spent most of the day on other engagements. But today was more interesting than most days because it was the last Friday of the month. Six years ago, when Raja promoted me to senior consultant, he identified me as someone he wanted to mentor to become a "king" like him. He set up monthly mentorship meetings, during which he advised me on a variety of subjects. In addition to advice, every month he would lend me one of the books that made it onto his list of the "greatest business books ever written." In the next meeting, we would discuss the book and he would give me a new book.

Our first book was Raja's favorite—Sun Tzu's *The Art of War*. His favorite quotation was "All warfare is based on deception," and he often repeated it.

Over the years we had studied and discussed several acclaimed business books. Prominent amongst these were Michael Porter's *Competitive Strategy*, Eliyahu Goldratt's *The Goal*, and Napoleon Hill's self-improvement classic *Think and Grow Rich*. But the ones that meant the most to me were the books written by Peter Drucker, the father of modern Management. I quickly became a big fan of his writings. In my office, I had several Druckerisms pinned to my bulletin boards.

As I stepped into Raja's office, I saw him wiping his desk with a disposable cloth. Raja was obsessed with cleanliness. He used a lot of paper napkins and cleaning materials. He always opened doors with a paper napkin. He never used a napkin more than once and his waste basket filled up quickly. Although athletic and well built, he was prone to falling sick, especially during stressful times.

To Raja's credit, the Characterra premises were the cleanest I had ever seen. Raja paid the cleaning staff double the industry average, with the mandate that they kept the premises up to Raja's high standards of cleanliness. Once, the cleaners had not performed their duties to Raja's standards and they got to experience Raja's wrath in the form of a loud, angry outburst in front of several Characterra employees. This included his "first and last warning" that he would fire them immediately if they ever slacked off again. I remember his words clearly: "I can find someone better and cheaper than you with a snap of my finger." That was five years ago. There was never a cleanliness related incident after that.

In private, after he had cooled down from his outburst, Raja offered me his advice.

"A king will always need a few donkeys to do some heavy lifting that is beneath his dignity," said Raja. "To get work out of donkeys, first give them carrots. If the carrots fail, make sure you use a stick. But, to win a war, it is not enough to have donkeys. The king needs horses. Some employees are like horses, productive and efficient at what they do. But these people also need to be managed like horses, by keeping a tight grip on the reins. If you don't control them, they will take you in directions you don't want to go."

Raja finished wiping his desk and looked up at me. "What did you think of *Winning*?"

"An excellent book," I replied. "Jack Welch is truly one of the world's greatest business leaders. Did you know that when he was the CEO of General Electric, he grew their market capitalization from $4 billion to half a trillion dollars?"

"Yes. Which part of the book did you find most interesting?"

"I thought his chapter on hiring was interesting. Welch didn't include a person's character or integrity in his list of criteria he uses for hiring people. In contrast, the last book I read by Peter Drucker said, "By themselves, character and integrity do not accomplish anything. But their absence faults everything else."[6]

"Interesting," said Raja, though his tone showed that he was not enthusiastic about that topic. "I was more interested in the concept of getting rid of the bottom 10% of your staff."

"Do you think that that is feasible?" I asked. "I mean, if it is done more than once, do you think it can negatively impact the morale of the staff?"

"I think only the poor performers would lose morale, making it easier for managers to identify them and get rid of them. Overall, the book has a lot of great information. But what I like best about it is the cover. Just take a look at it."

Raja pointed the book's cover at me. The word "WINNING" was written in capital letters under Jack Welch's smiling face.

"People say that you should not judge a book by its cover," Raja continued. "But how could you resist reading this book after reading its title and seeing Jack Welch's smile? Nothing matters more in life than winning business contracts and battles."

As our conversation continued, we discussed the various ideas Welch presented and compared them to those of other business gurus whose books we had studied before. Raja enjoyed these discussions. They helped him keep his mind sharp. In me he had found someone he could bounce ideas off of.

In the last few minutes of the meeting we discussed the projects I was working on. He mentioned that he had received feedback from the partner in Brazil that my work was thorough and impressive. He also gave me some feedback on the slide deck I had prepared for the Brazilian engagement.

"Slide eight needs revision," he said as he displayed it on his screen. "This is the most important slide as it summarizes the plan of action. It is too simple and easy to understand. I need you to add a few more boxes, arrows, and colors to make it a little more complicated and impressive. We are not being given big bucks for simple advice. The more complicated our solutions, the more we can justify our fees. The greater our fees, the more attention our clients will pay for our advice. It's a win-win situation. Does that make sense?"

"It does."

He then inquired about a business case for a new chemical factory to be constructed in a tribal region in India.

"I reviewed your analysis for the options we are considering for the new chemical factory," said Raja. "All three have favorable returns on investment and would be feasible. However, I noticed that you did not include the analysis for the fourth option we had discussed last week. I'm referring to the one in which the waste is disposed in the neighboring river and two lakes."

"As I mentioned earlier, I excluded that option because of the environmental and health hazards it involves. Five villages with many thousands of villagers would lose their access to drinking water and they may be vulnerable to other health risks as well."

This was not the first time Raja had asked me to analyze a scenario that was unethical. Since I became a principal consultant two years ago, I have had to do such an analysis seven times. In all seven cases I had felt reluctant, but I had always complied with Raja's request. I thought at first that Raja simply wanted to show the client that we had considered every option. I had trusted that even if the client wanted to pursue an option that violated environmental regulations or human rights, the authorities would never permit it.

However, in each case, these unethical options got approved by the authorities and our clients proceeded with them. I had recently learned that this was due to Raja's connections in politics and in the public sector. He was related to several politicians and public servants in various government agencies in New Delhi and other parts of the country. While I was crunching numbers, he would "pull some strings" and all kinds of questionable things would become legitimate. It was this factor, hard to replicate, that gave him a competitive advantage over other consulting firms.

"Health risks duly noted," said Raja. "But think of this as a hypothetical option and do the analysis anyway."

This time, I knew it would not be hypothetical. "I'm not comfortable presenting Option 4 to the client."

Raja looked at me intently. "I'm not interested in your discomfort," he said. "That is weakness."

"I—"

"Listen. I am Characterra's leader. That means I am the king. Do you remember our discussion on leadership versus management?"

"Yes."

"Tell me what the difference is between a leader and a manager."

"Leaders look up and outside the firm—at vision, strategy, external competitors, etc. Managers look down and within the firm—at costs, productivity, subordinates, etc."

"Right now you are a manager, Arjun, but I am investing in you so that one day you will become a leader. If you continue to grow your knowledge and skills under my mentorship, that day will come soon.

"Remember that business is war. In this war, we have warriors like you, allies like our clients, and enemies like our competitors and the competitors of our allies. We also have kings, like me, who lead the troops into battle. In order to win a battle, it is alright for a king to sometimes resort to questionable means. The results achieved justify the means employed. Does that make sense?"

"Yes."

"Good. Always remember that you are a warrior and Characterra is your battlefield. That's enough mentoring for today."

3. The King and the Warrior

I spent Saturday thinking about Option 4. Was Raja right that the world could be divided into allies and enemies? Raja had built himself an empire on the principle that business was war, but what about the villagers living in the vicinity of the chemical factory? They weren't allies or enemies. They were just people trying to live their lives. What right did we have to impose suffering on them? Options 1, 2, and 3 would still bring the client a sizable profit, even if the return on investment was lower.

I tried to convince myself that perhaps Option 4 would remain hypothetical this time. I tried to tell myself that it wasn't really my ethical responsibility to worry about it in any case. The client would have to approve the option, and then it would have to go before the authorities; surely, it should be on their conscience, not mine.

The next Monday started with my weekly team meeting with the seven senior consultants who looked to me for guidance. At Characterra, there was no formal organizational structure, with subordinates reporting directly to their managers. Tasks were assigned to people based on skills, knowledge, and the needs of the clients who engaged us on different projects. However, these seven senior consultants reported to me in the sense that I was responsible for their performance reviews and would advise them on any challenges they may have.

I had managed to build strong working relationships with these consultants and had encouraged them to collaborate with each other. The culture of our team was one of sharing, in which we all shared information with each other while acknowledging that information is an asset that grows when shared.

As soon as the meeting was over, I got a message from Raja to come to his office ASAP.

"Thanks for the analysis," he said. "I have had some preliminary discussions with the authorities and have learned that Option 4 will get approved. We will focus our presentation on this option since it is clearly the most profitable for our clients. I have also decided to give you more responsibility and an opportunity to take the next step up in your career. This is a large project that will bring us a lot of revenue. At tomorrow's presentation, you will present our recommendations after I have given some opening comments."

Raja always gave the important presentations for the large deals. He knew that I had been waiting for an opportunity to make the presentation for a project of this size. But today I was reluctant.

"Thanks for the offer," I replied. "I don't think I'm ready for this one. Maybe next time."

If there was one thing Raja hated in life, it was to have one of his "warriors" not accept an order. His tone suddenly changed from nonchalant to serious.

"Last week you were very eager to do this presentation," he stated. "Suddenly you are no longer interested. Is it because of your concerns for environmental and health hazards?"

"I just don't think I'm ready for this one."

"What a pity. This opportunity would have prepared you for your promotion."

"Promotion?" I asked, taken by surprise.

"I have spoken with the other partners. All are pleased with your progress. We have decided to create a new position for you. You will be Characterra's first associate partner. You will not have a share in the profits. But you will be eligible for a larger bonus and will be the first person we would consider should we wish to expand the partner base. In addition, we will send you abroad for twelve months on training—three months at each of our international offices. Abroad, you will report directly to the partner in charge and work on our most strategic projects. You will shadow the partners at every client meeting and they will mentor you as I have been mentoring you. Imagine yourself as a world citizen, living and working in New York City, Sao Paulo, Jakarta, and Shanghai. And I almost forgot to mention—the promotion comes with a generous 50% increase in salary."

I paused for a few seconds to digest the details of Raja's offer. I asked myself—'What is the price of one human's conscience? Am I a warrior for a worthy cause or am I a mercenary for hire?' It is one thing to do an analysis for a scenario that may cause harm to society and the environment. That, for the sake of my career I was willing to do, though reluctantly. It was a totally different thing to advise a client to proceed with an unethical course of action.

"Arjun," Raja continued with his sales pitch. "Understand that this experience will do you a lot of good. You have a lot of potential. You have many of the qualities necessary for the charismatic leaders the world so badly needs today. You are a fast learner, extremely intelligent, have excellent relationship-management and public speaking skills, and happen to be blessed with good looks. It is very important that a leader be good looking and well dressed. When a leader who is pleasing to the eyes speaks, the audience's ears open wider. You remind me of myself when I was your age. However, you have one weakness that is obstructing your path to greatness."

"What?" I asked.

"Good is the enemy of Great," he replied, quoting the opening lines of *Good to Great*, a best-selling business book. "You are too good. You lack the killer instinct. Fortunately for you, I know the cause of your problem and also the solution."

"What?" I asked again, now really curious.

"Were your parents of the spiritual type? Did they try to inculcate so-called good values in you, such as *ahimsa*, *satya*, and *atithi devo bhava*? Do you know what these words mean?"

"Yes, they did raise me with those values," I replied. "*Ahimsa* means to do no injury. *Satya* means truthfulness. And *atithi devo bhava* means that the guest is God."

"There is your problem—your belief in impractical notions of righteousness," said Raja. "Now listen to me very carefully, for I have traveled the world and learned many things in the process. I am an atheist, and proud of it. I don't believe in God or that any higher consciousness exists in the universe. For me the closest thing that comes to divinity is money. You could call me a 'moneytheist.'"

Raja took a thousand rupee note from his wallet. He held it in front of my face. I could see the kind, smiling face of Mahatma Gandhi.

"This note you can touch, see, and smell," he continued. "It is real. Money can buy you the best things in life. Most problems in life can be solved with money, and larger problems can be solved when you throw more money at them.

"I am successful today because I am a practical man, not burdened by thousands of years of mumbo jumbo and voodoo. Nonviolence and truthfulness are only practiced by activists and hippies. They are studied by academics and intellectuals who are too much into theory and out of touch with reality. Such concepts were created to give a false sense of hope to weak people who lack the strength to take matters into their own hands. In the real world, these notions serve no purpose. In five hundred years, such ideals will become the footnotes of history. In contrast, moneytheists like me are practical people. We know that the real world is a jungle in which every creature has to fend for itself. The tiger does not ask the deer, 'Hey, Mr. Deer, I'm hungry, may I please eat you?' He simply kills and eats."

These were harsh words that I found difficult to accept. However, I reminded myself that Raja must be onto something. He definitely was successful and rich. Over the years, I had visited his large home, seen his three chauffeur-driven luxury cars, and met five of his beautiful, young girlfriends.

"We have talked about the cause of your problem," Raja continued. "Your good nature rooted in your impractical belief in righteousness. Fortunately for you, I also have the solution to your problem. But before I give you the solution, I have some words of advice that it is in your best interest to memorize verbatim. **Contentment and compassion are destructive of prosperity. One who acts under the influence of these never obtains anything high.**[7] **Discontentment is the root of prosperity.**[8] Never be content with what you have. If you have a two bedroom condominium, be discontented and get a three bedroom house. If you have a three bedroom house, be discontented and get a four bedroom bungalow and a five bedroom mansion after that. The same principle applies to cars, yachts, planes, vineyards, and any object that gives you pleasure through your senses. The key to success is to let your discontentment fuel you to strive for bigger and better. Does that make sense?"

"Yes," I replied, waiting to hear his solution to my problem.

"Great. Now for the solution to your problem. This task will toughen you up and prepare you for your promotion. I'm sure you remember our acquisition of Singh and Patel Consulting three years ago?"

"Yes. We got some excellent clients and colleagues in the process."

"I acquired their firm for their clients. I never cared for the employees or for the old school mentality of the two founding partners."

I had high regard for Kamaljit Singh and Padma Patel, and had the good fortune of meeting both women on several occasions during the acquisition and subsequent transition of staff. Although Singh and Patel were both about sixty, I would not refer to them as "old school." They were hardworking and honest, and ran their firm as a supportive and cohesive unit in which employees were treated not as employees, but as members of a community. Their attitude and approach to business made them exceptionally successful with their clients, many of whom were family-run businesses from prominent Indian entrepreneurial and business communities.

The two founders' style of management and leadership contrasted starkly with Raja's warrior style. The employees of Singh and Patel Consulting were willing to go the extra mile. The firm functioned not as a bunch of individual workers, but as a cohesive team; a macro-organism in which the whole was greater than the sum of its parts. Singh and Patel had both been impressed with Raja's passion and enthusiasm. They had retired soon after the acquisition. But things changed under Raja's leadership. The morale of the acquired employees declined steadily and with it, their productivity. The income Characterra derived from these employees was lower than Raja's expectations and significantly lower than the income that Singh and Patel had been getting from the same people.

"Singh and Patel belonged to a different era," continued Raja. "There's one thing you don't know about the acquisition. They made me sign an agreement that I would not fire anyone from their team for three years. I'll never understand it—they weren't related to any of these people by either blood or marriage. Anyway, the good news is the agreement ended last week. With the acquisition, we received twenty-three employees, of which five left voluntarily over the last three years. Of the remaining eighteen, I have decided to keep three analysts and fire the other fifteen. The firing needs to take place this afternoon. I'm not going to be around because I have something I need to attend to. My task for you is that you will meet with each of these people and get them off our payroll. I will send you a file via email with all the details you will need to terminate them. You won't need more than fifteen minutes per person. Here's the list."

Raja spoke these words in a nonchalant tone, like he was handing me a grocery list—"two bags of brown rice—I don't like white rice—and don't forget the lentils need to be whole, not split." People's careers and lives were at stake, but to him they were machines, not humans—machines that must be disposed of as soon as they were fully depreciated and had no residual book value. I went through the fifteen names on Raja's list. They included two principal consultants, seven senior consultants, and six analysts. The principal consultants were the two star performers of Singh and Patel Consulting.

"Why must this be done today?" I asked.

"If they are on our payroll for another week, we will be legally obligated to pay them the yearly bonus. It is perfectly legal to fire them today and not pay them the bonus. I had taken these dates into consideration when I signed the agreement. Finish this quote—'The general who wins the battle makes many—?'"

"The general who wins the battle makes many calculations in his temple before the battle is fought. The general who loses makes but few calculations beforehand," I replied, quoting *The Art of War*.

"Brilliant. Any questions?"

"The two principal consultants are my peers and report directly to you. Would it not be more appropriate if you let them go?"

"Don't think of them as your peers. They are nothing more than two bottlenecks obstructing your path to greatness. Unblock your path and rise. Also, remember that I am the one firing them. I am the leader, devising the strategy. You are the manager, responsible for the execution. I repeat—compassion is destructive of prosperity. The world is a cruel place, in which goodness is not a source of strength but of weakness. In water you need to be like the shark and on land you need to be like the tiger. Firing these people will make you tougher. It is also a test. If you pass this test, you will prove that you are worthy of your promotion. And a final piece of advice regarding tomorrow's presentation and your concern regarding environmental and health hazards. **The attainment of success is the sole criteria that should guide the conduct of a warrior. Whether the**

means are righteous or unrighteous, what doubts can there be if you are performing the responsibilities of a warrior?[9] Take into consideration my advice and my offer."

The offer was very generous. People better qualified than me, with MBAs from the world's highest-ranked business schools and global experience at leading management consulting firms, would have quickly accepted this offer.

"Besides, don't forget that you are indebted to me," Raja said. "I gave you a job when you had no prospects. I trained you to be the warrior that you are. When the world ignored you, I believed in you. Make sure I do not regret that decision of mine."

I suddenly saw the situation with clarity. Raja had offered me the carrot, the promise of a significant promotion, and now he was using the stick, an emotional blow in the form of the reminder of my debt. He was treating me like I was a donkey. But he was also giving me the option to become a tiger.

I did not need to hear any more. I chose tiger.

"A 50% raise is good," I said. "But 80% would be great."

"Why?" he asked, raising an eyebrow.

"I know that my contributions to Characterra and its clients result in far greater income for each of the partners than the salary I make. And after my training abroad, I am confident that I will be more productive and effective."

"60%," was Raja's next offer.

"I'll meet you halfway—70%."

"Halfway would be 65%. Deal or no deal?"

"Deal," I replied, taking the printout of Raja's list. "By the close of business today, none of the people on your list will be working for Characterra. And tomorrow, I will give a presentation that will benefit Characterra tremendously."

4. Winners, Losers, and the System

I got back to my desk and scheduled fifteen one-on-one meetings of fifteen minutes each, starting at 11:45 a.m. and ending at 3:30 p.m. This was going to be an unpleasant exercise; one that I could do, but was reluctant to do. Before I started the task, I took a look at the motivational quotations that were pinned onto a board in my office. There were sayings by great Management teachers, like Peter Drucker; great self-improvement authors, like Napoleon Hill; and great leaders, like Mahatma Gandhi and Martin Luther King, Jr. Normally, these inspirational sayings made me feel strong and motivated. But today, I did not feel any connection to them.

The first person on Raja's list was Albert Thomas, who led the IT Support team. He was a jovial and friendly person who had helped me with a variety of technology related problems over the years. 'Why Albert?' I asked myself. I then remembered an incident that had occurred soon after the acquisition. Raja and I were at Albert's desk for something when we noticed him copying files from one location to another using DOS, a PC operating system that was widely used during the 1980s and 1990s. Raja was shocked to see Albert type out "copy" followed by the source folder\filename and the destination folder\filename. This task could have easily been done with a simple copy and paste or a drag and drop with minimal mouse clicks. As we walked away from Albert's desk, Raja shared his thoughts with me.

"DOS to copy files?" Raja exclaimed. "Seriously? Only old school dodos like Singh and Patel would have hired this guy. He belongs in Jurassic Park with all the other dinosaurs."

Apart from the fact that Albert often used DOS, his work was always efficient and we never received any complaints regarding the support he or his team provided to the other employees of Characterra. But I was not the leader. I was only the manager. And I had to complete the task Raja had given me.

I politely explained to Albert that I had been tasked to convey an unfortunate message to him and that effective immediately he was no longer an employee of Characterra. He was visibly distressed upon receiving this message. But he said nothing and asked no questions. He had worked with Singh and Patel for fifteen years before joining Characterra. He simply nodded his head to acknowledge that he received my message. Then he got up and left my office in a state of shock.

The next two happened to be two of the senior consultants who reported to me and had met me a few hours earlier under completely different circumstances. Letting them go was disheartening, given the friendships we had built over the years and the time and effort we had invested in building our team. I behaved professionally, keeping calm while also displaying sympathy for my former colleagues. They did not respond well. Neither had much to say, but I could tell by the looks on their faces that they felt deeply betrayed by me. I tried to remind myself that I was just the messenger, but the words felt hollow.

I let ten more employees go before facing the last two, the two principal consultants. They were my peers in rank though decades my senior in experience, education, and age. Both had Doctor of Philosophy (PhD) degrees and were professors at universities before they decided to join Singh and Patel Consulting. They liked to be referred to as professors.

My 3:00 p.m. meeting was with Professor Abhay Pandit, a marketing guru who was an expert on surveys and market research. Years of delivering lectures to young people had made him a vocal person who never hesitated to share his opinion. On several occasions in the past, he had fearlessly confronted Raja in public when he witnessed any form of injustice to Characterra employees. Raja had been waiting for the day he could get rid of the professor, who he considered to be less of a colleague and more of a competitor.

Professor Pandit allowed me to communicate the news of his termination of employment. After that he stayed silent for five seconds before giving me a piece of his mind.

"I demand an explanation," he yelled at me. "Explain to me the cause of my termination. Are you mindful of the contributions I have made to this firm and its clients? My annual reviews for all three years that I have worked here show that I met the expectations of my role. Has my work now become below expectations? If so, should I not get a warning and some feedback first?"

I patiently tried to calm him down, framing the dismissal in the words that Raja had instructed me to use.

"Characterra is reorganizing its structure to stay competitive in the market," I explained. "When an organization makes efforts to increase efficiencies and enhance effectiveness, some roles do get impacted. That's the way of the corporate world."

Professor Pandit did not buy my explanations.

"Impacted?" he exclaimed. "Spare me the corporate jargon and answer my questions."

He gave me a few seconds, but I could not give him an authentic reply.

"You have words but not the answers to my questions," he continued. "If you had a conscience, you would have been asking questions instead of being a blind follower. Like your mentor, you are cold, empty, heartless and soulless. If Raja thinks he has made the right decision, he has lost his intelligence. It's a real pity that all of you will realize my contributions only after I am gone."

As Professor Pandit left my office, I glanced at my clock. It read 3:14 p.m. I tried to prepare my mind for the second principal consultant, Professor Payal Khan, who liked to be called Professor Pi. But I could not control the thoughts that entered my mind over the next few seconds. Professor Pi was one of the most interesting people I had ever met. She was a kind, friendly woman in her mid-fifties who always had a smile on her face. She was a mathematical and financial genius who had been one of the star performers of Singh and Patel Consulting. Two years ago, when I was promoted to principal consultant, Raja had instructed her to train me on all her tasks. She happily took me on as an apprentice and let me accompany her to meetings where I could see her in action. She taught me how to do her work and shared with me the financial templates she had built over her career. Although a brilliant expert in her field, she was not a gifted speaker or presenter. Raja disliked her from the moment he first saw her. She liked to dress in colorful ethnic clothing with intricate embroidery. Raja wanted his consultants dressed in dark suits and plain shirts. She ignored his repeated hints to change her style. Once, in frustration, Raja had asked me, "When will she realize that this is a consulting firm and not the set of a Bollywood dance number?" He had also described her to me as "rough around the edges" and lacking the charisma required to be a leader.

A mathematical wizard, she got her nickname from her fascination for the number pi, often approximated to 3.14. At exactly 3:14 p.m. on every March 14th, she would send out an email to all Characterra employees in the Gurgaon office. In this email, she would invite everyone to celebrate "Pi Day" by joining her for pieces of pie that she had brought to the office kitchen. The pies were always made of the most exotic fruits and tasted absolutely delicious. With Pi Day, she was able to retain some of the spirit of teamwork that Singh and Patel had encouraged. More than anyone else on Raja's list, I felt anxious about letting Professor Pi go. She had been a great mentor to me. And, if I was honest, there was something deeper to my feelings about her.

Professor Pi reminded me a bit of my own mother, who used to work as a mathematics professor. Around twice a week, she would spend a few hours in the evening coaching my brother and me. I remembered an incident from my childhood when Karan had just started learning the concept of pi. For his calculations, he used the approximation of 22 divided by 7. Our mother did not allow us to use a calculator and encouraged us to do calculations mentally or on paper. She would often say, "If you use your mind, it will become stronger." At one point, Karan got frustrated of multiplying numbers by 22 and then dividing by 7. He asked our mother for a shortcut. She pulled out a book from our bookshelf called *The Trachtenberg Speed System of Basic Mathematics*. The author, Jakow Trachtenberg, was a Jewish mathematician who developed a system of mental arithmetic while he was imprisoned in a Nazi concentration camp during World War II.

One of Trachtenberg's techniques helped us perform more efficient calculations with 22/7. Instead of multiplying by 22, we doubled the number and then multiplied it by 11.

For example, 512 * 22 became 1024 * 11. Multiplication by 11 was easy, because all we had to do was add each digit to the one next to it on the right. So to figure out what 1024 * 11 was, we started with 4, then 2+4=6, then 0+2=2, then 1+0=1, and then finally 0+1=1, for a total of 11,264.

We still had to divide by 7, but the trick did prove to be a powerful shortcut. Within a year Karan and I had mastered all of Trachtenberg's techniques, which gave us a competitive edge in our future studies and careers.

But Karan and I were like most children. We were usually more interested in playing sports or watching television than studying. At these instances, our mother would sell to us the benefits of education.

"I will not force you to study," said mother once. "You cannot force anyone to be motivated to improve themselves. The motivation for self-improvement comes from within. That said, there are some things you must understand about the benefits of education. Around the time of India's independence from British rule in 1947, the average life expectancy for people was around thirty-five years. Your grandfather, my father, was born in British India. Like many in that era, he lost his father when he was only a child. His mother, who was uneducated, worked as a maid at the homes of various families in our ancestral village to pay for his school and expenses. For additional income, your grandfather at your age used to work after school as a delivery boy and waiter. He had no electricity at home, so he used to study under the streetlights on the village's main road.

"His hard work paid off. He went on to do a degree in civil engineering, moved from the village to a town, and had a career building bridges across India. A simple man, he always credited his success to the blessings of Goddess Saraswati, the Goddess of Learning. He made sure that my sister and I had the best education. If today I am a professor of mathematics, it is only because of his support and encouragement.

"Today, your father and I live in a large city and are able to pay for your education, so that you don't have to work to pay for it. The reason I'm telling you these stories is not to force you two to study out of guilt. It is to inspire you so that you are motivated from within to achieve greatness. In two generations, we as a family have progressed from a village to a town to a city, from poverty to a middle class lifestyle. All this was achieved through education. Think what you two will be able to achieve if you continue this tradition of education and progress."

I realized that my mind had digressed again. I reminded myself that I needed to focus on the task ahead. Professor Pi walked in at exactly 3:15 p.m. When I explained the reason for calling her in, she did not look surprised. I can only guess that she must have seen the others being escorted from the building and had deciphered that it was the Singh and Patel staff that was being terminated. But she was visibly upset.

"I should have seen this coming," she said. "That King of Deception, Raja, had this planned at least two years ago. No wonder he made me train you on most of my tasks. He said it was because we were going to grow and needed to strengthen our team. But that deceitful egomaniac just wanted to get rid of me. He looks smart and talks smoothly, but he is out of touch with reality.

"My student, here is your last lecture. Style can never be a substitute for substance. Dressing up in fancy suits and delivering presentations with colorful charts and catchy buzzwords may impress our clients but will not serve their needs. The advice that you should give the client is the advice that benefits the client. Not the advice that brings maximum revenue to the consulting firm, even though it may put the clients at a risk. Singh and Patel were successful because they invested in building relationships with their clients. They took the effort to understand their needs and advised them appropriately. They were able to earn the clients' trust because they had integrity, character, and humility. These are qualities that Raja either lacks or does not care for."

Professor Pi was making valid points. But I had made my choice. I would be a tiger. I would follow Raja into battle.

"That may be true," I said. "But Raja has turned Characterra into one of the most profitable consulting firms in India. I think the success of his strategies speaks for itself."

"And how long will it last? If you put clients at risk, will they come back to do business with you again? Will they recommend you to others? Is making money the only measure of success?" She gave me a piercing look. "You should be wary of following others blindly, Arjun. Do you realize that this is a great injustice to those who are losing their livelihoods today?"

"This is not injustice," I replied. "This is just business."

"Think. In addition to being former employees of Singh and Patel Consulting, what did the people who were let go have in common?"

I paused and thought for a few moments. Then it struck me. All were in their fifties. I wondered how I could have overlooked something so obvious. Was it the carrot, my promotion, or the stick, my indebtedness?

"You know it's an injustice," Professor Pi said. "I can see it in your eyes. You are a good person with a pure heart. You can be so much more than

31

Raja's warrior. You don't have to be an agent of pain and suffering. You can be an agent of happiness, kindness, and all that is good in the universe."

After the professor left, I stared blankly out of my window. Her words resonated with me. My father had been laid off around two years ago. He had worked for his company for twenty-five years. He had started as a chemical engineer and had made it to middle management. A consulting firm had come in to assess the workforce. The consultants had recommended that the firm let my father go, along with a dozen other middle managers. All were in their fifties. My father, who was fifty-seven years old at the time, wanted to work longer. He was devastated. The consultants had used the same words that I had just used with the Singh and Patel employees: "staying competitive," "increasing efficiencies," "enhancing effectiveness," "roles impacted," and so forth.

At that distressing time, it was my brother Karan who came to the rescue, flying in from New York on the earliest available flight. He bought my parents a retirement house in a posh neighborhood in Bangalore and convinced them to retire early and enjoy the good life. I have often wondered what happened to those less fortunate than my parents.

My thoughts were interrupted when I received a text message from Raja.

"Is it finished?" he asked.

"Yes," I replied.

In less than a minute, Raja sent out an email to all employees of Characterra. It had clearly been written earlier and had only now been sent out. In this he explained that we had a "reorganization" and a "reduction in force" to make Characterra more "competitive." He listed the names of all the people "impacted" by the reorganization. He mentioned my promotion and congratulated me for it. Around 7:00 p.m., when all of the other employees had left, Raja walked into my office carrying a bag. He took out a bottle of Scotch and my new name plate, which read "Arjun Atmanand, Associate Partner."

"I knew you would do it," he said. "I've had this plate sitting in my desk drawer for two weeks. Let me be the first to congratulate you."

"Thanks."

"And these are a signing bonus for the new Associate Partner," he said, handing me two boxes.

"Thanks again," I said, as I opened the boxes.

The first had a set of king and ace cufflinks, exactly the kind Raja had. The second had an impressive Rolex watch. My debt had just increased.

"Accessories fit for a future king," Raja added. "This calls for a celebration. Join me for some Scotch."

Raja had come prepared with two glasses and an ice bucket. He poured us both a drink and handed me a glass.

"Cheers," he said.

"Cheers."

"This one is an eighteen-year-old single malt Scotch. What do you think?"

"It's very good," I replied, after taking a sip.

Raja took a sip and went into a world of his own. It was quite obvious that he had already had a few drinks before coming to meet me. He held up his glass and started to ramble.

"Scotch and wine are two things that mature and improve with age," said Raja.

"And people?" I asked, remembering the Singh and Patel employees. "Do they not mature with age?"

"Unfortunately, they don't," he replied. "With age, passion is replaced by complacency and ambition for success is replaced by an acceptance of mediocrity. The process of maturing Scotch, however, increases its aroma, flavor, color, and smoothness. Smell it—it smells like the perfect combination of flowers, fruits, honey and the best aromas that nature has given us. Taste it—it tastes like the essence of nature was distilled over and over and over again, only to produce this nectar. See it—it looks like liquid gold. Drink it—its smoothness is unmatched."

He paused to take a few sips before he continued.

"A king needs to be a connoisseur of the fine things in life. He must have well-trained senses that should be able to distinguish between the refined and coarse things in life. You will soon be flying all over the world. When you return, you must bring me only bottles of single malt Scotch. I don't care for blended Scotch. By the way, how did your afternoon go? Did you enjoy firing people—the power, the exhilaration, and the boost to your ego?"

"It was an interesting experience," I replied. I had not found anything enjoyable in breaking peoples' spirits. But I didn't want to dampen Raja's mood.

"I can see that you are tougher already. You deserve your promotion."

Raja finished his drink and started pouring himself another.

"There is a subject I wanted to get your thoughts on," I said, as Raja started his new drink.

"Go ahead."

"You told me earlier that Option 4 will get approved by the authorities. I suppose that if it is approved by the authorities, it is technically legal. But what about ethics?"

"Ah, the 'E' word," Raja said with a sigh. "I had a feeling you would bring it up one day. I'm glad you are bringing it up today for I am in a happy mood. I'm going to resolve this doubt of yours once and for all."

He walked over to my window and took a look outside at the street and neighboring buildings.

"Our offices are clean," Raja said. "But take a look outside and you will see dust, dirt, pollution, poverty, and all kinds of other things that are displeasing to the eyes. This window is not an ordinary window. It is a transparent wall that separates the pleasant from the unpleasant, the clean from the dirty, and the rich from the poor. I'd rather stand inside this air conditioned office than be on the street. Do you see that beggar? The one who always sits across from this tower? From the street, that beggar looks like a man. From up here, he looks like the insect that he truly is."

After a few seconds he looked in my direction.

"You are so used to predicting the future and advising clients on how to proceed," he continued. "Do this and you will have a net present value of so much. Do that and you will get payback within so many months. But for questions about ethics, you need to look at the past, not the future. Do you know who I admire most in the history of the world?"

"Who?"

"The British ruling class." Raja paused to smile at me while I registered my shock. "Think about it. They were tigers among men. For centuries, the British nobles ruled over the lower classes in their own country. People with last names like Baker, Barber, Butcher, and Butler existed only to serve the upper class. And then things got disrupted with the Industrial Revolution. Suddenly the servants could leave their masters and join factories. Many rose up through the ranks and became wealthy in their own right. This gave rise to a third class in society, the middle class. The separation between the rulers and the servants now became blurry.

"When this happened the ruling elites came up with a brilliant idea— colonization. Why rule over the relatively few British common men when you can rule over millions of people in other countries? Why be limited to the scarce natural resources of a tiny island when you can plunder the abundant resources of continents?

"When the British came to India, the Indians, too good for their own good, practiced their 'guest is God' philosophy and welcomed the newcomers. The British ruling class took whatever they wanted. Within a couple of centuries, a once advanced and wealthy civilization was reduced to third world status. In 1700, India accounted for around a quarter of global GDP. By 1950, India's share of the global economy had fallen to 3%.

"In spite of all this unethical behavior, everyone still respects the British ruling class. The royal family is treated as celebrities and the royal weddings are viewed all over the world as grand spectacles. Nobody calls them thieves or pirates. None of the wealth or jewels they looted was ever returned to India or to any of the other countries in the world that the British colonized. And this will not change. Repatriation of wealth is impossible because it would be worth several times the GDP of the UK.

"So what does this history teach us? We must learn from the British ruling class and emulate them. Take wealth by whatever means necessary. Once you have wealth you can do whatever you want and everyone will treat you with respect."

Raja left the window and once again took a seat opposite me.

"Who are today's colonialists?" he asked, as he poured himself another glass of Scotch. "Those who take from others and get to walk away free of consequences or penalties?"

"No idea," I replied.

"Wall Street bankers," he explained. "Consider the global financial crisis that started in 2008. Hard working people all over the world lost their hard earned savings and retirement funds. The bankers made big bonuses and toasted each other with champagne to celebrate their magnificent gains. Then, when they could not pay their bills, the governments of the world bailed out these bankers using the taxes paid by the same hard working people who lost their own money. The bankers kept their bonuses and are respected as society's elite. Why didn't they pay fines or spend time in jail? Because their money paid for lobbyists, who bought the support of the politicians. No team that has the referee as their twelfth player can ever lose. The Wall Street bankers have all of the gains with none of the pain."

Raja then laughed. On most occasions, he laughed only after he had taken a few of drinks.

"Nothing good can come from being good," he said. "It is absolutely thankless. If you are good, people will take advantage of your goodness and think that you are a fool. If one day you need their help, they will forget all the good you have done for them and turn their backs on you. There is an incentive to following the law. If you break it and get caught, you might go to jail, or have to pay some penalties. But there is absolutely no incentive for being good."

He paused and took another few sips of Scotch.

"My mother used to tell me stories when I was a child," he continued. "After the stories she would talk about 'the moral of the story.' But these stories were fiction. When you analyze true stories from human history, from the British ruling class colonizing the world all the way to Wall Street gaining world supremacy, you find that the moral of these stories is that there are no morals in the world. There are only winners, losers, and the system.

"Winners are those who can manipulate the system to reach the goal of making money. The means employed, call them deception, loopholes, shortcuts, or by whatever name, are irrelevant as long as you don't get caught in the process. The system will not change. Only the players will be different, as will the winners and the losers. The system is truly magnificent. It is built on a foundation of deception and illusion. Commoners believe that it is an egalitarian system, that if you work hard you will be rewarded, that if you do good, good will happen to you. But the royals know that this is not true and see through the illusion. They manipulate the system for their own gains. But they do so without breaking the illusion, for it is the illusion that keeps the commoners from revolting and trying to change the system. Through this system, the rulers, who tend to be the top 1% of people in terms of wealth, become richer. Simultaneously, the bottom 99% get poorer, in the process destroying the middle class. The middle class, if destroyed, will not be missed. It is nothing but an anomaly, a byproduct of the Industrial Revolution, that disrupted the system. Make sense so far?"

"Yes," I replied, not being in the mood for a debate.

"Losers whine about the system," Raja continued. "Winners win by manipulating it. I don't see why people make a big deal about the corruption in India. Corruption is everywhere. In America they do it wearing suits and ties, smooth talking their way with a lot of class. Here, they do it wearing local attire and speaking a mix of local languages and broken English. They tell us directly how much we need to bribe them and we don't have to waste time beating about the bush."

Raja paused to take another sip of Scotch and give me time to absorb his teachings.

"What I have taught you is the royal mindset," he continued further. "It worked for the royals of the past and still works for the royals of today. I know that you are the descendent of common men. But I explain to you this key to riches because I see great potential in you. Trust me and follow my lead without questioning my judgment. Don't waste your time being too good for your own good. Concepts like ethics exist in myths and fairy tales to give a sense of hope to the masses. Those of the ruling class know that such notions are nothing but bottlenecks to greatness in the real world. I am not a dreamer. I am a visionary. I am building a global empire in the real world and you will be my right-hand man. Do you see my vision?"

"Yes," I replied.

"I'm glad we've got that clear," he replied nonchalantly. "A new chapter in your life begins tomorrow. Best of luck."

Raja finished his drink, got up, and left my office.

5. Arjun's Crisis

As I got ready for work the next morning, my mind was swirling. I was thinking about the presentation I had to give to the client. I was imagining the devastation that Option 4 would cause. I was thinking about what Professor Pi and the other Singh and Patel employees must be feeling this morning. I was thinking about the values my parents raised me with. Were they really just fairytales, as Raja had suggested? I was thinking about Karan, living his exciting, high-stakes, high-profits life on Wall Street. And Raja, with his flashy lifestyle and his provocative ideas.

I was finally back on a path to success. I was getting closer to achieving everything that I had thought I wanted. And yet I was feeling more confused and conflicted than I ever had before.

I need more time, I thought. I just need a little more time to think all of this through.

I looked at myself in the mirror wearing my red tie, white shirt, and black suit. And suddenly it occurred to me that I was living the "mirror test" that Peter Drucker had written about in the *Harvard Business Review*. "Ethics requires that you ask yourself, What kind of person do I want to see in the mirror in the morning?"

If I presented Option 4, would I still be able to look at myself in the mirror? Perhaps failing this test is the price one must pay for wealth and success.

I decided to stop over at a nearby park before heading to work, to get some time to myself and a change in location. The sun was beginning to rise. At the park I found an empty bench, sat down, and collected my thoughts as I watched the sky start to brighten.

I thought back to my conversation with Jyoti. I wondered if she was right, if looking back into my past could help me with the problems I was facing today. Her question suddenly entered my mind: "What could have happened around two years ago to trigger your dreams and poor sleeping habits?" It suddenly struck me what the event had been. Two years ago, Raja promoted me to principal consultant. Soon after that he had me working on unethical assignments that involved recommending questionable options to Characterra's clients. These options had magically gained the approval of the authorities due to Raja's relationships with influential people. And I had stopped sleeping peacefully at night.

I felt angry. Why had I not been able to get my student visa to the

United States? Why was I not now achieving great wealth on my own terms, like Karan? How was it possible that I had been distracted by a hallucination? Nothing like that had ever happened to me before or since.

As I sat on the bench, I battled my moral crisis caused by the doubts in my heart. Overwhelmed with conflicting thoughts, I was experiencing a rare dilemma in which I had absolutely no idea how to proceed. I resorted to an unscientific action I had not done since I became an adult. I said a little prayer in my mind: 'If there is any entity or higher consciousness in this universe, please help me now. I am in great need of some advice.' Shaking my head, I pulled my mind back to Earth. I glanced at my watch. It was 6:19 a.m.—time to head to work.

"Woof!" I heard the sound of a dog's bark.

Startled, my attention fell upon a soft golden light that was forming to my right. After a few seconds, I could see a man sitting next to me. I also noticed that he had a dog at his right.

"Namaste," said the man, with folded palms and a slight bow of his head.

"Namaste," I replied, using the same Sanskrit greeting, which means "the divine in me bows to the divine in you."

"Woof!" The dog barked again.

"Dog says Namaste," said the man.

"Namaste," I said to the dog, too startled to realize that I was addressing an animal.

The man had a clean-shaven face and head, and looked like he was in his early thirties. He also had a complexion like that of pure gold, with an aquiline nose and athletic build.[10]

The only piece of clothing he had on was a white *dhoti*, a traditional Indian garment that wraps around the waist and fully covers the legs. He was also wearing a rosary and a few bracelets, all made of *rudraksha* beads— seeds of great spiritual importance across many parts of Asia.

"Ah, sunrise!" said the man. "What a beautiful sight. It never ceases to amaze me."

"What is so great about it?" I replied. "It happens every day."

"One moment it is dark. And within minutes you are enveloped by golden light. From darkness you are led to light. You don't find that amazing?"

"It's ordinary. Like I said, it happens every day."

"Sometimes a thing is valued only if it is scarce or expensive. Sunrise, however, is common and free."

The man took a deep breath.

"Ah, the smell of fresh air," he said. "Another extraordinary thing. Though the pollution is quite high today. The air used to be so much cleaner."

"Cleaner air? Seriously? When was the air in an Indian city ever clean?"

"It was cleaner a few hundred years ago. And a few thousand years ago, it was even cleaner."

At this point I was amused. The man's mannerisms and clothing, along with the dog attentively staring at me, made me momentarily forget my immediate problems.

"And you were alive several thousand years ago to make that claim?" I asked.

"Yes," he replied.

"You are a funny man. And your words, clothing, and this dog are definitely intriguing. Who are you supposed to be?"

"What do you mean by 'supposed to be?'"

"Who are you?"

"You can call me Yogi."

"Alright, Yogi. I must admit I am impressed by your costume and the confidence with which you deliver your dialogues. You are a gifted actor."

Yogi gave me a confused look, like I was talking in some other language.

"You are not an actor?" I asked. "Anyway, I have a lot on my mind right now. I don't have the time to speak with you."

I looked at my watch. It still showed 6:19 a.m., and had stopped ticking.

"Strange, my watch has stopped," I said.

"Your watch is fine, Arjun."

"No, it stopped. I can see that it has stopped. How do you know my name? And why are you here, talking to me?"

"I'm here because you asked for advice. Didn't you ask for advice?"

"Yes, I did," I stared at him. I had not spoken my request out loud. "What's happening here?"

"All that you can perceive through your ordinary senses—all that you can hear, touch, see, taste, or smell—is part of the material world or plane of existence, composed of matter and objects. In the material world, all objects conform to the laws of time, space, and causation—as in cause and effect."

Yogi leaned over and picked up a stone beside the bench. He raised the stone in the air and then let it drop to the ground.

"In parallel," he continued, "there exists another world—one beyond the laws of time, space, and causation—that cannot be perceived by the ordinary senses. I will refer to this world as the spiritual world. Your watch has stopped because you have now joined me in the spiritual world. When this journey is over, you and your watch will once again conform to the laws of time, space, and causation."

I paused in disbelief for what felt like a few seconds.

"Are you a magician?" I asked. "Is this trick of stopping my watch a display of your *maya*, your power of illusion?"

"Do you know the difference between reality and illusion?" he replied.

"Yes. This does not seem like an illusion. Therefore, I must be sleeping and this must be a dream."

"Do you know the difference between one who is sleeping, one who is dreaming, and one who is awake?"

I pinched my forearm hard.

"When I pinch my arm, I can sense pain," I said. "I can also see the change in the color of my skin. Therefore, I must be awake. You are here to help me?"

"Yes," he answered. "I will give you a gift. You have to choose between two options. If you choose option one, I will answer your questions and give you advice. I will not tell you everything. But I will provide you with an education that will help you solve your current crisis. In addition, it will help you solve future problems by giving you a holistic way of thinking that, though ancient, will be new to you. The other option is that I will give you wealth equal to one thousand ounces of gold. Which option do you choose?"

Yogi demonstrated by materializing a gold coin from thin air, which he then moved through the air into my hand. It was an ounce in weight and of the purest quality possible for coins. Yogi's powers seemed authentic and I began to believe that he really wanted to help me.

"This is an amazingly brilliant coin," I said. "Its radiance is intoxicating. At the current value of gold, a thousand ounces is a large sum of money. I could probably quit my job and start my own firm." I thought about Raja. "You know, my boss would say that most problems in life can be solved with money, and that larger problems can be solved when you throw more money at them."

"And what would Raja say to one thousand ounces of gold?" asked Yogi.

"He would probably say, 'Make it one million.'"

"Very well. I will change your second option from one thousand ounces of gold to one million ounces of gold. Which option do you choose?"

The gold felt heavy against my hand. But the weight on my mind was heavier. "That is indeed a large sum of money. More money than I can possibly imagine. However, it is likely that I will continue to face dilemmas in the future that are similar to the dilemma I face now. For this reason, I choose the education."

I returned the coin to Yogi, who made it vanish.

"You have chosen wisely." Yogi smiled at me. "As it is written in the Upanishads: 'Both the beneficial [shreya] and the pleasurable [preya] present themselves to a man. The calm soul examines them well and discerns. He prefers the beneficial to the pleasurable; but the fool chooses the pleasurable out of greed and avarice.'"[11]

"The education I will give you will not give you the answer to your dilemma. Instead, it will teach you to elevate your thinking so that you will be able to solve various different kinds of problems you will face in the future and prevent those problems from becoming crises. Let us proceed."

The dog barked. Then the three of us were covered with golden light and transported through time and space. The golden light disintegrated over a span of what felt like around five seconds. I could now see our new surroundings. We were in a hall filled with several thousand people. Yogi and I were dressed as monks in orange robes. Most people were dressed in western clothing, but from another era.

"Where are we?" I asked.

"In Chicago, at the Art Institute," replied Yogi.

"When?"

"September 11th, 1893. We are attending the Parliament of the World's Religions. A brilliant Yogi and scholar is about to build a bridge between the East and West. He will introduce the Western world to Yoga and Vedanta. This is a turning point in human consciousness. On this day, the ancient philosophies and practices of the people of South Asia will be gifted to everyone on Earth."

Soon, a monk dressed in orange robes started to give a speech. I recognized him as Swami Vivekananda. He was a brilliant speaker who mesmerized the audience.

"Sisters and brothers of America," were the first words of the Swami's speech. These words were received by a standing ovation from the audience of several thousand that lasted for a full two minutes. He spoke of tolerance, universal acceptance, and the harmony of religions.

After his speech, Yogi, the dog, and I were transported to other days and places to hear the Swami's lectures on a variety of Yoga and Vedanta concepts.

During one of his lectures, he spoke about energy, matter, space, and other scientific concepts from the perspective of Vedanta. The man sitting next to me was paying great attention and making detailed notes and diagrams in his notebook. A quick glance at his book told me he was either a scientist or an engineer. He was clearly well versed in Sanskrit terminology because he was using Sanskrit words in his notes. At one point, he had a big smile on his face and a twinkle in his eye. Out of curiosity, I introduced myself to him after the lecture. I recognized him when he mentioned his name. He was Nikola Tesla, the great engineer who had many inventions, including the alternating current, induction motor, and radio, without which there could have been no wireless technology.

"*Akasha* (all-pervading space)! *Prana* (life-force energy)!" Tesla exclaimed as he waved his hands around in the air. "**If you want to find the secrets of the universe, think in terms of energy, frequency, and** vibration."

"I wanted you to meet Tesla," said Yogi, "to help open your mind to the education I am about to give you. I know that Tesla is a scientist whose work you admire. I wanted you to see that the ancient ideas developed in Yoga-Vedanta philosophies can provide powerful inspiration to the modern world."

At the end of the last speech that I attended, Swami Vivekananda got off the podium and walked past the audience. At one point he stopped in front of Yogi and me. He looked at me and said the most inspirational words I had ever heard: "**Awake, arise, and dream no more!**"

He then left our presence. The dog, who was standing beside Yogi and me throughout these speeches, then barked. Once again, the three of us were covered with golden light and transported through time and space.

6. From Knowledge to Wisdom

The golden light disintegrated and I could see our new surroundings. We were now in a beautiful forest full of tall trees laden with flowers and echoing with the delightful sounds of a variety of birds. The ground was covered with soft green grass upon which was spread a carpet formed of flowers that had fallen off the trees. I had never seen so much greenery in my life. Bees hovered around the flowers tempted by Mother Nature's nectar. Many species of birds of exotic colors were visible, including magnificent looking swans. Several deer roamed freely and without fear. Cool, scented breezes, conveying the fragrance of fresh flowers, blew in all directions.[12] I took a deep breath of the fresh air. For the first time in my life, I realized that air could be refreshing and energizing.

The sun had just risen and was painting the sky in a myriad of colors. Nearby, there was an amazingly beautiful lake. At a distance, I could see several tall mountains. The dog walked ahead and Yogi and I followed. I looked down at myself and saw that I was now dressed in a white *dhoti* similar to the one Yogi was wearing.

As we were walking, we crossed paths with a group of girls and boys around age ten. They greeted us in Sanskrit and with friendly smiles on their faces. They were walking in the direction of a nearby village that was becoming visible beyond the trees. They seemed like students who were heading to school. I could also see some of the inhabitants of the village. They were dressed in simple pieces of cloth, some white and some saffron colored.

We walked a little further and reached the lake. It was covered with lotuses and large swans. I stopped in awe. I had never seen a more beautiful sight. Only Mother Nature could have orchestrated this harmonious symphony of sunlight, mountains, lake, trees, animals, birds, insects, and flowers. Here she was at her finest.

"Where are we?" I asked.

"In a forest close to the Himalayas," replied Yogi.

"When?"

"Around three or four thousand years before your time."

In the lake I saw a swan a few feet away eating something it had found near a lotus.

"The swan (*hansa*) and the lotus (*padma*)," said Yogi. "Both are important symbols of Vedanta. The swan used to be a frequent visitor to the land of Bharat, the ancient South Asian subcontinent."

"What's their symbolism?"

"Observe the swan."

The swan was eating a white, sap-like substance that was coming from the plant and spilling into the water.

"The swan has the power of discernment (*viveka*)," said Yogi. "It can discern between the milk-like sap and water, consuming the sap while not consuming the water. Milk symbolizes that which is pure. Through discernment, one can understand the difference between purity and toxicity, between righteousness and unrighteousness."

The swan took flight. While taking flight, water from its webbed feet fell upon the lotus leaf.

"Now observe the lotus," said Yogi. "The water that falls on the lotus leaf flows off again and back into the pond. The lotus is a symbol of purity. It blooms in muddy waters. But its leaf has the ability to remain unaffected by the water. The world is filled with purity and toxicity. The lotus reminds us that one must be pure in spite of being surrounded by toxicity."

We walked on to reach the village.

"What is this place?" I asked.

"It is a place of learning where many gurus run their residential schools. It is also inhabited from time to time by sages who visit to exchange ideas with the gurus and other sages."

I observed our surroundings as we walked through the settlement. Several teachers were conducting classes with various groups of students. Male and female students were grouped together based on their age. Classes started with students the age of five and went up to students the age of twenty. Subjects studied included philosophy, mathematics, economics, grammar, science, astronomy, and medicine. Classes were conducted under trees. I watched as children of all ages asked questions and contributed toward the conversations.

"This is the model of the Upanishads," continued Yogi. "Students are encouraged to think for themselves and ask questions. If you read the Upanishads, you will see several examples of how students learn by asking questions. If students simply memorize and blindly follow what is said by teachers and parents, their minds will not mature and their Intellects will not awaken. Those who cannot think for themselves will not be able to innovate and create new ideas for the benefit of the environment, society, their organizations, and themselves. They will only be fit for copying the creations of others. Those who blindly follow can neither lead nor manage others."

Elsewhere, students were chanting various mantras in Sanskrit.

"Independent thinking is done in addition to the memorization of important concepts that have been summarized over time into verses," said

Yogi. "You may have heard the following verses, which are from the Upanishads."

I listened to the verses being chanted:

Asato ma sad gamaya
Tamaso ma jyotir gamaya
Mrityor ma amritam gamaya
Om shanti shanti shanti
—Brihadaranyaka Upanishad 1.3.28

"Yes, I have heard them," I replied. "What do they mean?"
Yogi explained the meaning:

From the unreal, lead me to the real,
From darkness, lead me to light,
From mortality, lead me to immortality,
Om peace, peace, peace.

We also passed students doing deep breathing exercises (*pranayama*) and various yoga postures (*asanas*). At a distance, we could see students and sages sitting cross-legged in meditation.

"A healthy body," Yogi continued, "helps the learning process and promotes spiritual advancement. Breathing and exercise prepares the aspirant for meditation. Theory learned in the class is built upon by experimentation. There must be a balance between knowledge (*jnana*) and action (karma)."

The dog, Yogi, and I stood under a tree at the edge of the settlement and viewed the activities as a whole.

"Have you read the Bhagavad Gita?" asked Yogi.
"No."
"Why?"
"I am not into spirituality. I believe in science."
"Then why did you pray for advice?"
"I don't know why I did that."
"Yours is a problem shared by many youth of your time. In the name of science, you have turned your back not just on spirituality, but also on the philosophies that deal with Dharma (righteousness, duty) and *moksha* (the realization of spirit). I am now going to give you a gift. The wise have said that the best of all possessions is knowledge."[13]

A book made of ancient paper materialized in Yogi's hand. He took the book and tapped it on my forehead at the point between my eyebrows. The book disintegrated into a golden light that flew into my head through my forehead. For a few moments, I was blinded. Only when the light started to disappear did I regain my vision. I was breathless, sweating, and about to lose my balance. The dog barked and pointed its nose at a bench that had materialized behind me. I sat down and tried to control my mind, which was ablaze with countless thoughts.

"You now have in your mind all seven hundred verses of the Bhagavad Gita," said Yogi. "You know each word of the Gita in Sanskrit, along with its translation into every language you speak. Soon you will learn the relevance of the Gita to modern life, particularly to work and management. And in your own mind you will devise ways in which these teachings can be taught and applied to the world of business."

The verses flew through my mind. There were countless instances of words, such as "knowledge," "action," "wealth," "duty," "charity," "education," and other words relevant to management and leadership in the modern world of business. There was a universalism, interconnectedness, and inclusivity to the teachings of the Bhagavad Gita that extended not only to humans, but to all livings beings in the universe. I realized that to put a "religious" label on the Gita does a great disservice to humanity. If it was to fall under any category, spirituality would be the most accurate one.

"This book is deep," I said, after much contemplation. Meanwhile, another bench materialized opposite me and Yogi sat on it.

"Yes," Yogi added. "All humans can benefit from reading it. But the people who will gain the most from it are those who possess a mature mind and a pure and awakened Intellect."

"How do I cultivate a mature mind? How do I know when my Intellect has been awakened?"

"An awakened Intellect is one that can discern between purity and toxicity, like the swan and the lotus. To mature your mind, you must first learn about the five sheaths of the human body and how they interact with the world. The five sheaths are explained in the Upanishads.[14] The sheaths, ordered from the outermost to innermost are:

1. Physical or food (*anna*) sheath – *Annamaya kosha*
2. Life-force (*prana*) or breath sheath – *Pranamaya kosha*
3. Mind (*man*) sheath – *Manomaya kosha*
4. Wisdom (*vijnana*) sheath – *Vijnanamaya kosha*
5. Bliss (*ananda*) sheath – *Anandamaya kosha*

"Can you recall verse 3.42 of the Bhagavad Gita?"
The verse entered my mind:

The senses are said to be superior to the body; the mind (*man*) is superior to the senses; the Intellect (*buddhi*) is superior to the mind; and that which is superior to the Intellect is He (the Atman).
—Lord Krishna in the Bhagavad Gita, 3.42

"Do you understand now?"

"I think so. It would help if I could visualize this."

A pad of paper and a box of markers materialized in Yogi's hands. "Imagine these sheaths as five concentric spheres or circles," Yogi said as he passed me the materials. "The sheaths are similar to the layers of an onion. When you peel off one layer, there is another layer underneath."

I closed my eyes and imagined what this would look like. If Raja had asked me to make a slide for a presentation, what would I create to communicate the concept? I looked at the blank paper in front of me and began to draw.

Five Sheaths of the Human Body (partial)

Yogi looked at the page and clapped his hands with delight. "Yes! Exactly. The outermost sheath is the physical sheath. This sheath is the physical body that you can perceive with your senses of sight and touch. It is the densest and firmest sheath and possesses the most 'form.' Each sheath within it is more subtle and has less form. Think of them as having five grades of density, going from dense to subtle, from form to formlessness.

"All forms of matter have the physical sheath, and with it **material consciousness**, manifested as internal and external vibrations. As life evolved on Earth, organisms developed additional sheaths. In addition to the physical sheath, plants have the life-force sheath and with it **breath consciousness**. In this sheath lie the senses, by which one can hear, touch, see, taste, and smell. **The senses provide perceptions, including pleasure and pain, by sending inputs from the external world to the mind.**

"In addition to the life-force sheath, animals have a mind sheath. The mind is called *manas* in Sanskrit and is referred to simply as '*man*' in modern Indian languages. The word '*man*' sounds not like man, but like human. In contrast to other animals, humans have a sheath within the mind sheath called the wisdom sheath, which gives them the ability of higher thinking and discernment. The Intellect exists within this sheath. **The mind is the seat of impulsive thinking, while the Intellect is the seat of intelligence.**

"The Intellect is called '*buddhi*', a word that is related to 'Buddha' (the awakened one). An awakened Intellect can discern between righteousness (Dharma) and unrighteousness, and between purity and toxicity. Humans also have a sheath within the wisdom sheath called the bliss sheath. The bliss sheath gives humans the ability to experience pure bliss (*ananda*) or inner peace (*shanti*) from realizing one's Atma (soul, true Self). Within the bliss sheath lives the Atma, which is not a part of the five sheaths of the body. Imagine this Atma as a light bulb, a source of light or consciousness that vibrates through all five sheaths and makes the body a living organism."

I added a light bulb to my image.

"What is this life-force that exists in the second sheath?" I asked.

"This life-force is called *prana* in Sanskrit," said Yogi. "*Prana* is a life sustaining force or energy. Without it, the body would not be living. The energy of the sun, radiated in its rays, is an example of this force."

"I have often heard the phrase 'body-mind-spirit,'" I said. "Is Atma the spirit?"

"The ancient sages made a distinction between the material body that the senses can perceive and the unseen entity that makes the body alive," replied Yogi. "In Sanskrit, the term Atma refers to the soul, spirit, or Self that resides in the body of every living organism, including plants and animals. The term 'Mahatma' translates to Great (Maha) Soul (Atma).

"Earlier, I had spoken with you about two worlds or planes of existence that existed in parallel, the material world and the spiritual world. The material world has matter and objects that you can perceive through your senses. Think of this world as the one given to you by Mother Nature (*Prakriti* in Sanskrit). To perceive matter or nature, the mind focuses externally or outwards through the senses. The spiritual world, however, exists within. To perceive this, the mind needs to withdraw the senses and look within, in the direction of the Atma. The Atma can be realized through Yoga and meditation."

I took a few seconds to understand these concepts.

"What is the difference between mind and Intellect?" I asked.

"The senses pull the mind toward the external (material) world," explained Yogi. "The Intellect can, through discernment, Yoga, and meditation, focus on the internal (spiritual) world. Let's take the case of an individual addicted to tasty, but unhealthy, foods. When the individual perceives this type of food through the senses of smell or sight, the mind is drawn to it and tries to convince the individual to get it. A weak Intellect will succumb to the demands of the obstinate mind and get what it desires. However, a strong Intellect will be able to discern between healthy and unhealthy foods, and would have the discipline to control the mind. Through practice, the Intellect can control the mind, helping the individual get over such addictions. Think of this as an awakening of the Intellect and the maturing of the mind."

"I'm beginning to understand your explanation," I said. "**The Intellect is a subset of the mind, a portion within the mind that is capable of advanced thinking and discernment.** Is that why you told me to imagine the five sheaths as concentric circles, instead of as a hierarchical pyramid?"

"That's correct," answered Yogi. "Each sheath is a subset of the sheath that covers it. Each sheath is less dense, more subtle, and operates at a higher frequency than the sheath external to it. For this reason, the inner sheaths are capable of greater and more subtle functions."

"I understand that the five sheaths together make up the body," I said. "Also, that the inner three sheaths make up the mind. Why is the mind considered a subset of the senses, which in turn is a subset of the body?"

"Review what the Gita has to say on this topic."

Verses that addressed my question entered my mind.

"There are several verses in the Gita that refer to the mind as a sense," I said, after reviewing the verses. "In verse 10.22, Lord Krishna states that 'of the senses I am the mind,' implying that the mind is the most superior of the senses. In verse 13.5, he talks about the 'senses and the one (mind).' Also, in verse 15.7, he states that the Atma draws to itself 'the (five) senses with mind for the sixth.' It follows that **the mind is a subset of the senses**. How can the mind become a sense?"

"Six is the number of the senses,"[15] answered Yogi. "Ignorant people think that only the external world is capable of gratifying the senses, and are blind to everything else.[16] The mind can become a sense when the other senses are drawn within, so that they no longer focus on the external (material) world. In a state of stillness, when the five ordinary senses are not used, the mind behaves as a sixth sense. Think of it as a third eye that is placed on your forehead, between your eyebrows. When this third eye is opened it can perceive the spiritual world, which the ordinary senses cannot perceive. In a balanced state, such as during meditation, the mind can become attuned to the Atma. When in resonance with the Atma, the mind can intuitively gain access to infinite sources of information."

"The mind becomes a sixth sense through intuition," I reiterated. "Swami Vivekananda mentioned this in one of his lectures."

"All knowledge that the world has ever received comes from the mind; the infinite library of the universe is in your own mind."
—Swami Vivekananda[17]

"So, in a Zen state of mind, I too will be able to access information from the infinite library of the universe?"

"Yes, you will be able to when you are in a yogic or meditative state. In fact the Japanese word 'zen' was derived from the Chinese 'chán,' which was derived from Sanskrit '*dhyana*', which means meditation. Buddhist monks took meditation and related practices from ancient South Asia to other parts of the world. The Zen school of Buddhism was created by Bodhidharma, a prince of the Tamil Pallava dynasty who moved to China and lived there for the rest of his life."

"Is there a difference between what one perceives from the external and matter facing ordinary senses and what one perceives from the internal and Atma facing mind as the sixth sense?"

"Review what the Gita has to say on the topic of knowledge (*jnana*)."

Many verses related to knowledge entered my mind.

"The Gita uses multiple words to describe knowledge," I said. "Lord Krishna talks not just about *jnana*, but also about other words rooted in '*jna*,' including '*ajnana*,' '*vijnana*,' and '*prajna*.'"

"That is correct," said Yogi.

"*Ajnana* is the opposite of *jnana*," I deduced. "It can be translated as 'ignorance,' the opposite of knowledge."

"Yes, it is ignorance that causes much of the pain, suffering, and toxicity on Earth. When we speak of darkness, we are referring to ignorance. The wise have said that the world is enveloped with ignorance. It is ignorance that does not permit a thing to show itself."[18]

"That would explain two of the four words derived from the same root," I replied. "However, *vijnana* and *prajna* are more complicated. With regards to *vijnana*, I am reminded of two of India's highest civilian awards—the Padma Bhushan and the Padma Vibhushan. Of the two, I am aware that the Padma Vibhushan is the higher and more prestigious award. It seems that the prefix 'vi,' when added to a word, makes the word relate to something higher. By this logic, *vijnana* would mean wisdom or more advanced knowledge. This would also be consistent with the wisdom sheath (*vijnanamaya kosha*) being a subset of the mind sheath (*manomaya kosha*). I'm beginning to understand *jnana* as knowledge and *vijnana* as wisdom. So, is wisdom a subset of knowledge, just as the Intellect is a subset of the mind?"

"Yes," replied Yogi. "That would be an explanation that the world of business would be able to understand. **Wisdom (*vijnana*) is a subset of knowledge (*jnana*), just as the Intellect (*buddhi*) is a subset of the mind (*man*). All wisdom is knowledge. But not all knowledge is wisdom.**"

"Yogi, what then is *prajna*?" I asked.

"The prefix 'pra,' like 'vi,' denotes something higher," explained Yogi. "Think of 'pra' as related to prime, premium, or supreme. *Prajna* is more subtle than *vijnana*. It transcends the material world and the external facing ordinary senses. *Prajna* is perceived through intuition, through the sixth sense focusing inward, facing the Atma and the spiritual world. Thus you have the answer to your question regarding the difference between what one perceives through the ordinary senses and the extraordinary sixth sense."

In my mind I linked *prajna* to the third eye, using which the mind can perceive, through intuition, that which the ordinary senses cannot.

"If *prajna* is more subtle than *vijnana* (wisdom) and is perceived through intuition, would it be accurate if I called it 'intuitive-wisdom?'" I asked.

"Yes," replied Yogi.

"So, is intuitive-wisdom a subset of wisdom, just as the bliss sheath is a subset of the wisdom sheath?"

"Yes. **Intuitive-wisdom (*prajna*) is a subset of wisdom (*vijnana*). All intuitive-wisdom is wisdom. But only wisdom that is gained intuitively by focusing on the Atma and internally toward the spiritual world can be properly called intuitive-wisdom.**"

"I understand your explanation of the three levels of knowledge," I said. "But can you help me apply these insights to the business world?"

"Let's start by discussing terms you use regularly," suggested Yogi. "What do data, information, and knowledge mean to you?"

"The term data means 'something given' and is plural for the Latin word '*datum*,'" I replied, happy that I knew the answer to Yogi's question for a change. "Data can be in the form of numbers, text, images, and other input that are processed by humans or computers to produce information. Information is derived from the Latin word '*informare*,' which means 'to give form to.' I think of information as 'data put in formation that makes sense.' I often use information to create reports. I think of knowledge in terms of the words of a great Management teacher, Peter Drucker. He had said that 'knowledge is information effective in action, information focused on results.'"

"Does the term '*datta*' mean anything to you?" asked Yogi. "Think of Verse 1.15 from the Bhagavad Gita. In this verse, Prince Arjuna blows his conch shell, which is named '*devadatta*.' The conch shell is a shell of great importance in Dharma traditions. It is often used as a wind instrument, blown like a trumpet. '*Devadatta*' is derived from '*deva*' (God, divine) and '*datta*' (given, gift) and translates to 'God-given' or 'divine gift.'"

"Sanskrit '*datta*' and Latin '*data*' both mean 'given,'" I exclaimed as I linked these two fundamental concepts.

"Good observation," said Yogi. "We have linked knowledge (*jnana*) to the mind (*man*), which lies in the mind sheath. Similarly, we have linked wisdom (*vijnana*) to the Intellect (*buddhi*), which lies in the wisdom sheath, and linked intuitive-wisdom (*prajna*) to the bliss sheath, which is the closest to the Atma and spiritual world. How would data (*datta*) and information relate to the five sheaths?"

"Data would be linked to the outermost sheath, the physical body that comes in contact with the material world," I replied after some thought. "Information, which is data put into a formation that makes sense, would be linked to the second sheath. In this—the life-force sheath—lies the senses of perception through which one can hear, touch, see, taste, and smell. It also follows that **information is a subset of data, just as the senses are a subset of the physical body. All information is data. But only data that has been put into a formation that makes sense, can be called information. Similarly, knowledge is a subset of information, just as the mind is a subset of the senses. All knowledge is information. But only that information that has been applied for results can be called knowledge.**"

I looked down at the image I had sketched and I added 'data' in the physical sheath, 'information' in the life-force sheath, 'knowledge' in the mind sheath, 'wisdom' in the wisdom sheath, and 'intuitive-wisdom' in the bliss sheath.

Five Sheaths of the Human Body

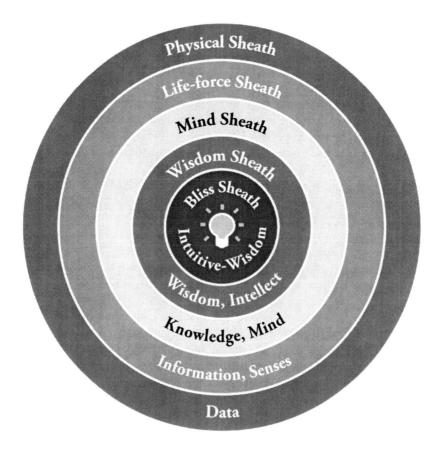

"We discussed that knowledge is applied for results," I said. "But then what is wisdom and intuitive-wisdom applied for?"

"For this you must learn about the four values or purposes of life (*purusharthas*)," said Yogi. "The four values are:

1. Dharma (righteousness, duty)
2. *Artha* (wealth, prosperity)
3. *Kama* (pleasure, desire)
4. *Moksha* (realization of Atma/Self, liberation, salvation)

"'*Artha*' translates to wealth or material prosperity. The world of business is well aware of the importance of wealth. '*Kama*' translates to desire or the pleasure that is derived through the senses. This word is quite well known in your time because of the *Kama Sutra* text. However, '*kama*' is not restricted to sexual desire or pleasure. It refers to all kinds of desire and pleasure, including that gained from the enjoyment of art and entertainment, or from eating delicious food. Wealth and desire are easily translated and understood. However, Dharma, which is of greater importance than these two values, is more subtle and difficult to translate. Dharma can be accurately translated as righteousness, duty, justice or virtue. The three values of *artha*, *kama*, and *moksha* have their foundations in Dharma.[19] It is Dharma that supports all creatures."[20]

"Does Dharma mean 'law?'" I asked.

"Sometimes Dharma is translated as law," replied Yogi. "However Dharma is greater than law in the civic sense. A certain deed may be legal, but it may not be ethical or just. Dharma goes beyond law and is closer in meaning to ethics and justice. Dharma is the foundation on which society is built.

"I will give you an analogy to help you visualize this. Think of society as a structure like a bridge or a building, with people and other living organisms as the bricks that make up the structure. The structure (society) is held together by Dharma, which is the foundation (righteousness) upon which the structure is built, as well as the cement—the duty of the individual bricks to bear the weight of, and contribute to holding up, the structure. For balance and harmony in society, the pursuit of wealth and enjoyment of pleasure must both be firmly rooted in Dharma. The wise have said that it is the righteous upon whom both the past and future depend."[21]

"*Kama* (pleasure) is derived from the senses," I said. "Knowledge, which is linked to the mind, is information that has been applied for results or *artha* (wealth, prosperity). Dharma is more important to society than the values of pleasure and wealth. Can Dharma be linked to the Intellect and wisdom?"

"Yes," replied Yogi. "Wisdom is linked to duty. True ignorance consists in not knowing one's duties.[22] One is to be called learned who knows one's duties."[23]

"We have determined that **knowledge (*jnana*) is the subset of information that is applied for results (*artha*)**. It follows that **wisdom (*vijnana*) is the subset of knowledge that is applied for righteousness (Dharma)**."

"Woof!" barked the dog, as it wagged its tail in happiness.

"An important righteous activity is philanthropy (*dana*)," said Yogi. "Another way to think of this is that, **while the mind utilizes knowledge for prosperity, the Intellect utilizes wisdom for philanthropy**."

I paused for a few moments to think about how these concepts applied to my work at Characterra and to my crisis, in particular. Many questions came to my mind. Was my duty to make money for Raja? Or was it to make money for Characterra's clients? Or did my duty extend to others, including the villagers and other living beings that would be impacted by the environmental and health hazards of the recommended Option 4? I could apply my knowledge for results and wealth for Raja and the clients by recommending that option. In the short term, there would definitely be benefits to be gained. But would that be the best option for the long term? I thought back to Professor Pi's advice about cultivating relationships with clients. Could recommending Option 4 lead to reputational risks or to legal ramifications for Characterra and its clients? If so, was it really the best strategy for these stakeholders?

Yogi's explanations were making me think, and I started to believe that if I continued to understand his teachings, I would be able to solve my crisis. I thought back to my mentorship sessions with Raja and wondered if the distinction he drew between management and leadership could be connected to the framework Yogi was explaining.

"Would it be accurate to link knowledge to management and wisdom to leadership?"

"No. Both categories of workers need both knowledge and wisdom. Leaders tend to have greater responsibility, and hence should possess more wisdom, but not all who lead have wisdom. There are several instances of tyrants who have been successful leading others down a path of unrighteousness. Unrighteous leaders lead to suffering. In contrast, all living beings benefit when people are led by righteous leaders."

Raja was clearly a leader and was leading the employees, including myself, toward his vision of building an empire. Those who did not share his vision and those who did not fit in with his plans would be eliminated, as the Singh and Patel employees had been. He was knowledgeable and successful. But was he wise? He was building his empire on the foundations of *artha* and *kama*, but what about Dharma? And how did *moksha* fit in?

"Please tell me about the fourth value, *moksha*," I requested.

"*Moksha* is more subtle than the other three values," replied Yogi. "It translates to the experience of realization of Atma/Self, liberation, or salvation."

"Would it be linked to the innermost bliss sheath and intuitive-wisdom?"

"Yes. **Humans have the ability to experience pure bliss (*ananda*) or inner peace (shanti) from *moksha* (the realization of Atma).** The wise have said that peace of mind is the highest object, for prosperity proceeds from that quality.[24] However, different scholars will often have their own interpretations regarding the distinction between wisdom and intuitive-wisdom. At this depth within the five sheaths, we are dealing with subtle concepts and the lines can get blurry. What the mind perceives when it acts as the sixth sense can be applied to different values. But it is sufficient to understand that wisdom obtained through intuition can lead to the experience of *moksha*."

"Then it follows that **intuitive-wisdom (*prajna*) is the subset of wisdom that can lead to the experience of realization (*moksha*).**"

I looked back down at my drawing of the five sheaths of the body. Yogi was adding more and more layers to this simple diagram. I decided I needed to summarize these concepts in the form of a table to help me link the sheaths of the body with the corresponding subsets of data. The senses, mind, Intellect, and bliss sheath can, respectively, serve the purposes of **Perceptions, Prosperity, Philanthropy,** and **Peace,** by the means of **Inputs, Impulses, Intelligence,** and **Intuition.** Information, knowledge, wisdom, and intuitive-wisdom can respectively be applied for **Reports, Results, Righteousness,** and **Realization.**

Sheath of body	Purpose served	Means utilized	Subset of data	Application
Bliss sheath	Peace	Intuition	Intuitive-wisdom	Realization
Intellect	Philanthropy	Intelligence	Wisdom	Righteousness
Mind	Prosperity	Impulses	Knowledge	Results
Senses	Perceptions	Inputs	Information	Reports

"You have learned many concepts since we met," said Yogi. "When you received the Bhagavad Gita, you learned every word in Sanskrit along with its translation into all the languages that you speak. Think of the Sanskrit words as divine data (*devadatta*) and of the translated verses as information that makes sense to you. You have mentioned that you have often used information to create reports. When you apply this information for results (wealth) it becomes knowledge. When you apply this knowledge for Dharma (righteousness, duty) it becomes wisdom. Intuitive-wisdom is a subset of wisdom, gained through intuition, that can lead to the realization of Atma.

"I can see that it helps you to understand concepts by writing them down. I suggest that you arrange these concepts into a mantra built on the verses from the Upanishads. Do you remember the mantra that you heard students chanting when you walked around these schools? Start with these verses, and then add 'from ignorance, lead me to knowledge, from knowledge, lead me to wisdom.' As we proceed, and as you take in new concepts, keep adding lines to this mantra."

I took out a fresh page and wrote:

From the unreal, lead me to the real,
From darkness, lead me to light,
From mortality, lead me to immortality,
From ignorance, lead me to knowledge,

From knowledge, lead me to wisdom…

"These words are good, Yogi, but I think I need to develop a set of principles or more detailed instructions in addition to the mantra, so that I can better remember and apply your teachings."

"That is also a good idea. What will your first principle be?"

I thought about it for a moment, and then I wrote:

Through meditation and intuition, use your mind as a sixth sense to access the infinite library of the universe.

"Excellent," said Yogi. "Reality, light, and immortality are important concepts that we will discuss further as we proceed with our conversations."

7. Reality-Consciousness-Bliss

"We have spoken about two worlds existing in parallel," said Yogi. "I mentioned that in the material world, which is given to you by Mother Nature, all objects conform to the laws of time, space, and causation—as in cause and effect. This world is perceived by focusing the senses externally. In contrast, the spiritual world is beyond the laws of time, space, and causation. To perceive this, the mind needs to withdraw the five ordinary senses and look within—internally, in the direction of the Atma. In this internal direction, past the five sheaths, lies an absolute, supreme reality that is called 'Brahman.' Brahman is the 'Soul of the Universe', the eternal, infinite, indivisible Atma or One that lives in all living beings. The Atma and Brahman are united. The Atma is Brahman. This is the core principle of *Advaita* (non-duality) Vedanta. All living organisms are interconnected, and are part of the One, the supreme macro-organism. There are several verses in the Gita that explain Brahman and the oneness of all life."

Relevant verses entered my mind, some of which were:

With the heart concentrated by Yoga, with the eye of evenness for all things, he beholds the Atma in all beings and all beings in the Atma.
He who sees Me [Lord Krishna as an incarnation of Brahman] in all things, and sees all things in Me, he never becomes separated from Me, nor do I become separated from him.
He who being established in unity [Oneness], worships Me, who am dwelling in all beings, whatever his mode of life, that Yogi abides in Me.
—Lord Krishna in the Bhagavad Gita, 6.29-31

Beyond Me, O Dhananjaya [Prince Arjuna], there is naught. All this is strung in Me, as a row of jewels on a thread.
—Lord Krishna in the Bhagavad Gita, 7.7

"In the Rig Veda, the oldest of the Sanskrit scriptures, there is a magnificent statement," said Yogi.

Truth is one, sages call it by various names.
—Rig Veda, 1.164.46

"Swami Vivekenanda talked about this, too!" I suddenly realized. "In his first speech at the Parliament of the World's Religions he said, 'As the different streams having their sources in different places all mingle their water in the sea, so, O Lord, the different paths which men take through different tendencies, various though they appear, crooked or straight, all lead to thee.'"

"Indeed," said Yogi, his eyes twinkling. "Consider another related verse from the Upanishads:

He, the One and Undifferentiated, who by the manifold application of His powers produces, in the beginning, different objects for a hidden purpose and, in the end, withdraws the universe into Himself, is indeed the self–luminous – May He endow us with clear Intellect!
—Svetasvatara Upanishad 4.1

I found this verse truly fascinating. Brahman was the being that produced the entire universe from itself and then withdraws the universe back to itself. This sounded a lot like the Big Bang Theory.

"Think now of light and consciousness," said Yogi. "It is for this reason that I spoke with you about Brahman. You have visualized the Atma as a light bulb at the center of the five sheaths that illuminate the body. This Atma is the source of consciousness in the form of light that vibrates through all five sheaths and makes the body a living organism. In the same way, Brahman, the 'Soul of the Universe', illuminates all beings in the universe with consciousness."

Another verse from the Gita entered my mind.

The light which, residing in the sun illumines the whole world, that which is in the moon and in the fire – know that light to be Mine.
—Lord Krishna in the Bhagavad Gita, 15.12

"Brahman, the supreme macro-organism, is the source of an infinite, all-pervading 'Universal Consciousness,'" said Yogi. "At the other end of the spectrum, you have individual organisms that have consciousness of their own. All material objects have consciousness in the form of vibrations. Plants are beings that have, in addition to material consciousness, an ability to breathe. Animals are more conscious and have minds that let them think like individuals. However, they lack the intelligence of humans and behave impulsively and instinctively."

In my mind, I related material consciousness to the outermost physical sheath, breath consciousness to the life-force sheath, and individual consciousness to the mind sheath.

"Understand that with each additional sheath, consciousness expands,"

Yogi continued. "At one end of the spectrum of consciousness (light), you have matter with material consciousness. On the other end, you have Brahman, the source of a consciousness so infinitely expansive and all pervading, that we can best call it Universal Consciousness. The more advanced a being is, the more expansive will be its consciousness. You can also visualize these stages of consciousness in terms of the colors that make up the visible spectrum. Material consciousness is represented by red. Each stage of higher consciousness will be represented by a color of higher frequency than the color before it. For now, think in terms of five stages of consciousness, like the five sheaths, and assign the colors red, orange, yellow, blue, and violet. These colors are linked with the Seven Chakras, a concept I will explain later to you."

I looked back at the concentric circles I had drawn and realized that I had intuitively colored them according to the spectrum that Yogi had just described.

"Those who have realized the Atma have experienced oneness with Brahman and have described it as Reality-Consciousness-Bliss (*Sat-Chit-Anand*)," said Yogi. "**Sat-Chit-Anand describes Brahman as a supreme Reality (*Sat*) that is beyond change, an infinite all-pervading Universal Consciousness (*Chit*) that is beyond space, and an eternal Bliss (*Anand*) that is beyond time.** This experience of oneness is referred to as immortality. Here are some verses from the Upanishads that explain this concept."

Beyond the senses is the mind, beyond the mind is the Intellect, higher than the Intellect is the Great Atman, higher than the Great Atman is the Unmanifest.
Beyond the Unmanifest is the Person [*Purusha* or Brahman], all-pervading and imperceptible. Having realised Him, the embodied self becomes liberated and attains Immortality.
His form is not an object of vision; no one beholds Him with the eye. One can know Him when He is revealed by the Intellect free from doubt and by constant meditation. Those who know this become immortal.
—Katha Upanishad, 2.3.7 to 2.3.9

I linked immortality to the realization of Atma and the experience of bliss. I was finally starting to understand why the students were chanting about being led from the unreal to the real, from darkness to light, and from mortality to immortality.

"I see a large gap between individual consciousness and Universal Consciousness," I said. "Is there a being that exists between the individual human and universe as a whole?"

"Yes," replied Yogi. "A great macro-organism exists between the human and the whole. It is a living, breathing, conscious organism that also meditates. I have mentioned the material and spiritual worlds. In Yoga-Vedanta there exist three worlds or planes of existence—material plane (Earth, *bhur*), intermediate plane (atmosphere, *bhuva*), and spiritual plane (Heaven, *swaha*). Consider the following verses."

Earth meditates, as it were. The mid-region meditates, as it were. Heaven meditates, as it were. The waters meditate, as it were. The mountains meditate, as it were. The gods meditate, as it were. Men meditate, as it were. Therefore he who, among men, attains greatness here on earth seems to have obtained a share of meditation. Thus while small people are quarrelsome, abusive and slandering, great men appear to have obtained a share of meditation. Meditate on meditation.
—Chandogya Upanishad 7.6.1

"The Earth is that macro-organism?" I asked.

"Yes," replied Yogi. "It is a macro-organism made up of all living beings on Earth. It has a consciousness of its own. You can call it 'Earth Consciousness.' This consciousness is greater than the individual consciousness of a human, but lesser than the Universal Consciousness of Brahman. You can also link Earth Consciousness to wisdom that the Intellect can understand. This differentiates it from the intuitive-wisdom that is gained from meditation and intuition, through which Universal Consciousness can be realized. **True wisdom is displayed when a being lives in harmony with the Earth.**"

"Modern science does not consider the Earth to be a living being."

"Some scientists of your time subscribe to the holistic view that the Earth is alive and is a single self-regulating system. They refer to this theory as the Gaia Theory, named after Gaia, the Greek Earth-goddess."

"The theory does not seem scientific."

"Science has its limitations."

"Please explain."

"Scientists rely on their five ordinary senses and on their tools for their observations," Yogi explained. "Since these senses have their limitations, tools of greater sophistication need to be invented. A few centuries before your time, microscopes helped scientists discover micro-organisms and telescopes helped them discover distant objects in space. As the tools became more accurate, they were able to discover more objects that, until then, they never knew existed. These objects were always present, but were not perceivable through their tool-enhanced senses. Undiscovered objects still exist. Scientists, however, are limited to their tools. Maybe someday all scientists will think that the Earth is a macro-organism. For now, understand that science does have limitations."

I realized that I was going to need a more elaborate chart to contain and connect these various factors. I took a new piece of paper from the pile Yogi had given me and began to draw using the same colors as before to show the progression from one end of the spectrum to the other.

"Yogi, what you're talking about could be called the Reality-Consciousness-Bliss framework," I said, and showed him what I had drawn. "See? The rightmost column is inspired by the five sheaths of the body, and explains the human purpose or value that each sheath can serve. The senses, mind, Intellect, and bliss sheath can, respectively, serve the purposes of **Perceptions, Prosperity, Philanthropy,** and **Peace**, by the means of **Inputs, Impulses, Intelligence,** and **Intuition**. The leftmost column is inspired by the five subsets of data. Information, knowledge, wisdom, and intuitive-wisdom can, respectively, be applied for **Reports, Results, Righteousness,** and **Realization**."

"Yes," smiled Yogi. "Very good."

I then added 'Earth Consciousness' to the Reality-Consciousness-Bliss framework. I also assigned milestones to the framework, starting from 0.0 and going all the way to 5.0. The material plane was at the 0.0 milestone and the spiritual plane at 5.0. Data, material consciousness, and the physical sheath of the body start to take form at 0.0 and complete at 1.0. Higher stages of consciousness are similarly linked to higher milestones. The transformation between knowledge and wisdom happened between 3.0 and 4.0. This corresponds with the expansion from individual consciousness to Earth Consciousness. True wisdom was displayed when the being's consciousness was at 4.0, or Earth Consciousness.

Looking at the framework I had just drawn, I began to wonder about how consciousness could be both individual and collective.

"Are there other macro-organisms out there?" I asked Yogi.

"You yourself are a macro-organism."

"What?"

"Yes. Within the human body there are trillions of bacteria and other micro-organisms. Many have a beneficial symbiotic relationship with the body, such as the intestinal flora that aid digestion and other functions. Others have no effect and some may be disease causing."

Yogi paused for a few seconds and then pointed at the sky above the lake. A flock of swans were flying in a V-shaped formation. It was a magnificent sight.

Reality-Consciousness-Bliss Framework

Atma (Soul) or Spiritual/Internal World		
Reality *(Sat)*	**Consciousness** *(Chit)*	**Bliss** *(Anand)*
Subset of data and its **Application**	Stage in the evolution of Human Consciousness	Sheath of Body, its **Purpose** and its **Means** of utilization

5.0

Intuitive-Wisdom *(prajna)*	**Universal Consciousness**	**Bliss** *(Anand)*
Intuitive-Wisdom *(prajna)* is the subset of wisdom that can lead to the experience of **Realization** *(Moksha)*; by which Reality *(Sat)*, which cannot be perceived by the ordinary senses, is known	I realize that the Universe's living beings are all ONE with *Brahman* (the eternal, infinite and never changing Soul of the Universe)	The seat of **Intuition** and the sub-portion of the mind that provides the experience of Bliss and inner **Peace** *(Shanthi)*

4.0

Wisdom *(vijnana)*	**Earth Consciousness**	**Intellect** *(Buddhi)*
Wisdom is the subset of knowledge that is applied for **Righteousness** (Dharma)	I understand that Brahman lives in all living beings on Earth; and that the Earth with all of its inhabitants is one living, breathing, conscious macro-organism	The sub-portion of the mind that is the seat of **Intelligence** and has the ability to discern *(viveka)* between righteousness (Dharma) and unrighteousness *(adharma)*; can be utilized for **Philanthropy**

3.0

Knowledge *(jnana)*	**Individual Consciousness**	**Mind** *(Man)*
Knowledge is the subset of information that is applied for **Results** *(artha)*	I think that I am alone, separate from all living beings	Mind faces the ordinary senses and is the seat of **Impulses**; can be utilized for **Prosperity** *(artha)*

2.0

Information	**Breath Consciousness**	**Senses**
Information is data put in formation that makes sense; applied to create **Reports**	Consciousness from breath	Provide **Perceptions** including pleasure and pain, by sending **Inputs** from the material/ external world to the mind.

1.0

Data *(datta)*	**Material Consciousness**	**Physical Body**
Data are sensory inputs 'given' by Nature or the Material World	Consciousness from vibrations of matter	The vehicle of the Atma in the Material World

0.0

Nature *(Prakriti)* or Material/External World		

"The V-shaped formation allows the flock to travel greater distances," said Yogi. "The swan at the front gives an aerodynamic lift to those directly behind it, who in turn give a lift to those behind them. When the leader is tired it goes to the end of the formation and another takes its place. Together, the swans are able to travel further than if they had each flown independently. The whole becomes greater than the sum of its parts. Here you see a display of wisdom. Sometimes this can be seen in the animal kingdom, in spite of the fact that these creatures lack the Intellect of humans. The animals are able to display wisdom from their instincts. Together, these swans behave like a macro organism, capable of achieving more than would be possible by a lone swan."

"The Gita says 'Indivisible, yet It exists as if divided in beings,'"[25] I said. "I understand that the flock of swans has a consciousness greater than the consciousness of individual swans. This should also be the case with all groups and teams, if the members are able to collaborate and cooperate with each other. Would this be the case for humans working in organizations?"

"If a team of individuals can contribute and achieve more together than the sum of what each individual team member can do, then it would be accurate to describe the team as having a consciousness of its own," replied Yogi. "The tree that stands alone, though gigantic, strong, and deep-rooted, has its trunk soon smashed and twisted by a mighty wind. Those trees, however, that are close together are better able, due to mutual dependence, to resist winds that are more violent."[26]

This analogy made sense to me. In the Knowledge Age, work is often done by teams composed of workers with specialized knowledge, such as subject matter experts. In order for such teams to be effective, individual team members need to collaborate with each other and share their knowledge and skills. An effective team is able to contribute and achieve more through collaboration than the sum of all the contributions and achievements of each individual team member working independently.

I was reminded of how Singh and Patel's management style encouraged collaboration and teamwork. Employees were productive and engaged when managed this way. But this approach to management contrasted starkly with Raja's approach. Under Raja's way of management, the same employees who were productive under Singh and Patel became less productive.

"In that case, several levels of consciousness are possible," I said. "If groups of beings collaborated and cooperated with each other they would display a form of group consciousness. Beyond individual consciousness, there could be team consciousness, departmental consciousness, organizational consciousness, conglomerate consciousness, industry consciousness, and so on till you have Earth Consciousness. Similarly, cities and nations could have their own consciousness. Since individual consciousness is linked to knowledge and Earth Consciousness to wisdom, there would be several levels of wisdom that are linked to the levels of consciousness I have just mentioned."

I listed these levels as various milestones between knowledge (3.0) and wisdom (4.0):

4.0 Earth Consciousness (wisdom)

...

3.5 Industry Consciousness
3.4 Conglomerate Consciousness
3.3 Organizational Consciousness
3.2 Departmental Consciousness
3.1 Team Consciousness
3.0 Individual Consciousness (knowledge)

As I listed these milestones, I was reminded of the Japanese concept of keiretsu. This is a group of organizations that collaborate together and are closely connected via strong relationships and joint ownership. Such a group of collaborating organizations would fall beyond organizational consciousness (3.3) and nearer to conglomerate consciousness (3.4).

"Yogi," I said. "These ideas on consciousness make me recall a quotation from Einstein:"

"A human being is a part of the whole, called by us 'Universe,' a part limited in time and space. He experiences himself, his thoughts and feelings as something separated from the rest—a kind of optical delusion of his consciousness. This delusion is a kind of prison for us, restricting us to our personal desires and to affection for a few persons nearest to us. Our task must be to free ourselves from this prison by widening our circle of compassion to embrace all living creatures and the whole of nature in its beauty. Nobody is able to achieve this completely, but the striving for such achievement is in itself a part of the liberation and a foundation for inner security."
—Albert Einstein

"Very wise," said Yogi. "This quote is compatible with the philosophies of the ancient sages. However, while the physical universe that Einstein was referring to is limited by time and space, Brahman, the Soul of the Universe is beyond time and space. Through Yoga-Vedanta it is possible to widen your circle of compassion to embrace all living creatures.

"A macro-organism or group, be it the Earth or a team, is of greater importance than the individual. The Mahabharata tells us that an individual should be cast off for the sake of the family; that a family should be cast off for the sake of a village; that a village should be abandoned for the sake of the whole country; and that the Earth (material world) itself should be abandoned for the sake of the soul."[27]

I thought for a few moments on how this would apply to organizations and teams. It follows that if there is a toxic individual in the team, a person who may be talented but brings down the team's performance, that individual should be either reassigned to another team or removed from the organization.

"I am beginning to understand that an awakened Intellect and a mature mind can lead us from knowledge to wisdom," I said after some thought. "Our consciousness expands from individual consciousness to Earth Consciousness when we apply wisdom for righteousness instead of knowledge for material results. True wisdom is displayed when human consciousness has expanded to include the whole Earth and all beings that make up the Earth."

Yogi nodded his head in agreement. I summarized this concept in the following principle.

Mature your mind and awaken your Intellect by cultivating wisdom and expanding your consciousness.

"We have discussed many topics that are core concepts in Yoga-Vedanta," I said. "I wish to link these to the subject that is referred to in my time as Management."

8. Management Redefined

"What does Management mean to you?" asked Yogi.

"Management has been described in many different ways," I replied. "The description that means the most to me was given by Peter Drucker, who stated that 'the essence of Management is to make knowledge productive.' This is very relevant to the time I come from, which is often referred to as the Knowledge Age, an age in which knowledge is a key resource. The period before this was referred to as the Industrial Age, an age in which work was done primarily by the human hand and the operation of machines. **In the Industrial Age, the instrument of manual work was the hand. In the Knowledge Age, the instrument of knowledge work is the human mind.**"

"You have spoken about how 'data' and 'information' were derived from Latin. Do you know how the word 'management' was derived?"

"Yes," I replied, after remembering something I had once read. "The word 'management' is derived from Old French '*manège*' ('the handling or training of a horse'). The French word originates from Italian '*maneggiare*' ('to handle'), which in turn comes from Latin '*manus*' ('the hand')."

"You live in the Knowledge Age," said Yogi. "If you are from an age in which the instrument of work is the mind, why do you associate management with the hand (*manus*)?"

"I never asked myself that question," I replied, as thoughts entered my mind. "Not hand, but mind. Not Latin '*manus*,' but Sanskrit '*manas*' or '*man*.'"

We had discussed that an awakened Intellect and a mature mind can lead a human from knowledge to wisdom. I quickly wrote down the new definition of Management that was forming in my mind:

Management Redefined for the Knowledge Age

"Management" is '*man*' (mind) plus 'agement' (making mature). Management is the act of making knowledge productive by maturing the instruments of knowledge work—the minds of the people involved in the work.

"Yes, that is a sound definition," said Yogi. "Remember that 'age' is not the same as 'maturity.' As the Mahabharata tells us, one is not old because one's head is gray. But the divine regard her or him as old who, although a child in years, is yet possessed of knowledge."[28]

"A valid point," I agreed. "Hence the 'agement' in 'management' refers to mental maturity and not to physical age. On the subject of mental maturity, I have often faced a challenge as a knowledge worker. With so many things happening in life and work, it is difficult to control the mind and to stay focused. Why?"

"It is because you are dealing with something that is fleeter than the wind and with things that are more numerous than the grass in a field."

"What is fleeter than the wind?" I asked.

"The mind is fleeter than the wind."

"And what is more numerous than grass?"

"Our thoughts are more numerous than grass.[29] We have spoken about the hierarchy of body, senses, mind, Intellect, and Atma," continued Yogi. "I will now give you an analogy that will help you better understand what you are dealing with. Have you seen the image of the *Gita Updesh?*"

"Yes," I replied.

A famous image entered my mind. I visualized a chariot with white horses, with Lord Krishna as the charioteer and Prince Arjuna as the rider. This is the most famous image associated with the Bhagavad Gita and the Mahabharata. Although I had seen it in many forms of artwork, I had never learned the depth of its symbolism.

"The Gita and Mahabharata were authored by the great sage Veda Vyasa," said Yogi. "He was an advanced Yogi and a scholar of Vedanta. He wrote these texts and put ancient traditions in the form of stories. These were entertaining and at the same time explained ancient philosophies and practices. Many verses in the Gita are summarizations and explanations of concepts discussed in the Upanishads. The image of the *Gita Updesh* is inspired by the following verses from the Upanishads."

Know the Atman to be the master of the chariot; the body, chariot; the Intellect, the charioteer; and the mind, the reins.

The senses, they say, are the horses; the objects, the roads. The wise call the Atman - united with the body, the senses and the mind - the enjoyer.

If the *buddhi* [Intellect], being related to a mind that is always distracted, loses its discriminations, then the senses become uncontrolled, like the vicious horses of a charioteer.

But if the *buddhi* [Intellect], being related to a mind that is always restrained, possesses discrimination, then the senses come under control, like the good horses of a charioteer.
—Katha Upanishad, 1.3.3 to 1.3.6

"The body is the chariot, the vehicle used by the Atma for the journey of life," explained Yogi. "The horses symbolize the ordinary senses of perception. Through the senses, one can hear, touch, see, taste, or smell objects, which are symbolized by the roads. Some objects are important while others are distractions. An immature mind is overwhelmed by the multitude of inputs being sent through the senses. It cannot discern between what is beneficial and what is merely pleasant. Among the six senses, the mind that is easily moved is the most dangerous.[30] An immature mind is obstinate—like a child that keeps screaming and crying till it gets what it wants. The mind's role is to rein in the senses. The true power of the mind can be harnessed by the Intellect. An Intellect that does not control the senses through the mind is ineffective—like a sleeping charioteer who lets the horses run wherever they want. An awakened Intellect can make the mind mature and rein in the senses to take the chariot in the direction beneficial to the Atma, the passenger of the chariot."

Yogi paused for a few moments to let me understand his explanations.

I was reminded of Raja's advice that some employees were like horses, productive and efficient at what they did. He had advised me that these people needed to be managed like horses, by keeping a tight grip on the reins. This approach contrasted with Yogi's, in which the senses were the horses that needed to be controlled.

There was a striking contrast between the two understandings of Management. In *manège*, the focus is on controlling another animal or person. In the chariot analogy, the focus is on controlling one's own mind (reins) and senses (horses), while also factoring in the roles of the Intellect (charioteer) and Atma (passenger).

As with our other discussions on Yoga-Vedanta, the focus was directed inward from the body toward the Atma. This shift in focus had parallels with the advancements made in the study of Management. In the Industrial Age, scholars studied the behaviors of commodities and objects, as did prominent economists. With scholars like Frederick Taylor, father of scientific management, the focus went from the objects to the functioning and movements of the human body, particularly the hand. With Drucker, the focus went a layer deeper, to the study of the behavior of people. The chariot analogy looked at the full picture, linking the objects with roads, body with chariot, senses with horses, and mind with reins.

The advancements in Management followed the same progression of focus as Yoga-Vedanta, from the external/material plane to the internal/spiritual plane. The next advancement in Management would be a shift from knowledge to wisdom, brought about by a mature mind and an awakened Intellect.

"After learning the chariot analogy, what strikes you the most about the image of the *Gita Updesh*?" asked Yogi.

"Amazing," I answered. "Lord Krishna is the charioteer navigating Prince Arjuna in a great war between righteousness and unrighteousness. The Intellect is the charioteer navigating the Atma in the journey that is life. The Intellect must be like the Lord—pure and divine."

"Well said," replied Yogi. "Do you now have an idea why you often have challenges controlling your mind?"

"Yes. The mind is difficult to control because it faces the senses, which pull it toward objects that are pleasurable."

Relevant verses from the Gita then entered my mind:

Notions of heat and cold, of pain and pleasure, are born, O son of Kunti [Arjuna], only of the contact of the senses with their objects. They have a beginning and an end. They are impermanent in their nature. Bear them patiently, O descendant of Bharata [Arjuna].
That calm man who is the same in pain and pleasure, whom these cannot disturb, alone is able, O great amongst men, to attain to immortality.
—Lord Krishna in the Bhagavad Gita, 2.14, 15

"The human mind is a very powerful instrument," continued Yogi. "It, like fire, can illuminate if it is steady and controlled. But it can also burn and destroy if it is unrestrained. The following is an apt description from the Gita."

'As a lamp in a spot sheltered from the wind does not flicker,' – even such has been the simile used for a Yogi of subdued mind, practising concentration in the Self.
—Lord Krishna in the Bhagavad Gita, 6.19

"May I summarize this concept in the following principle?" I asked Yogi.

Channel the fire of your mind toward illumination, not toward ignorance or destruction.

"Yes," said Yogi. "Yoga-Vedanta philosophy also links the mind with fire, the third of the five great elements (*mahabhutas*). These are, in order from the subtlest to the most dense, space (*akasha*), air, fire, water, and earth. Note that the elements are elements of vibration. They differ from the chemical elements that matter is composed of. They go from formlessness toward having form, from the spiritual plane toward the material plane, and from higher frequencies of vibrations toward lower frequencies of vibrations. They are summarized in a sentence from the Upanishads."

From the Atman was born *akasha* [space]; from *akasha*, air; from air, fire; from fire, water; from water, earth.
—Taittiriya Upanishad, 2.1.3

"This sentence is followed, in this Upanishad, by several verses that explain the five sheaths of the body that we have already discussed," continued Yogi. "Each element is related in terms of vibratory frequency to each sheath. *Akasha* (space) is linked to the innermost bliss sheath, which is closest to the Atma. Air is linked to the Intellect and wisdom sheath. Fire is linked to the mind and mind sheath. Water is linked to the senses and life-force sheath. And finally, earth is linked to the physical body and physical sheath."

I was excited by the connections Yogi was drawing for me. The mind as fire made an excellent analogy. The mind controlled by a steady Intellect would be a channel of positivity, light, and illumination. An uncontrolled mind and unstable Intellect would lead to ignorance and darkness if the fire is put out, or to destruction if the fire is uncontrolled.

"The five elements are linked with five attributes," continued Yogi. "Space, air, fire, water, and earth have their respective attributes of sound, touch, vision, taste, and scent. Every one of these elements possesses, in addition to what is especially its own, the attribute or attributes of those coming before it.[31] *Akasha* is linked to sound and the sense of hearing. Air is linked to the senses of hearing and touch. Fire is linked to hearing, touch, and vision. Water is linked to hearing, touch, vision, and taste. The densest element, earth is linked to the five senses of perception: hearing, touch, vision, taste, and smell."[32]

I pulled out another piece of paper from the stack Yogi had given me. I need to visualize the connections between all of the analogies that Yogi was making:

Vibratory Element	Sense of Perception	Sheath of Body	Chariot Analogy
Space (*Akasha*)	Hearing	Bliss sheath	Not applicable, but Atma is the rider
Air	Touch, hearing	Intellect (*buddhi*)	Charioteer
Fire	Vision, touch, hearing	Mind (*man*)	Reins
Water	Taste, vision, touch, hearing	Senses	Horses
Earth	Smell, taste, vision, touch, hearing	Physical body	Chariot, Atma's vehicle for journey of life

The concept of *akasha* as an all pervading space linked to sound rang a bell in my mind. The first word that Nikola Tesla had said to me in Chicago was "*Akasha!*" Perhaps he was excited because this concept was consistent with the view that signals and energy could be transmitted across distances wirelessly.

"As the verse from the Upanishad suggests, the subtle is the cause and the dense is the manifestation," said Yogi. "An unsteady mind can lead to a diseased body. As a hot iron bar immersed in a jar of water makes the water hot, so does mental grief bring on bodily agony. And as water quenches fire, so does true knowledge allay mental agitation. As the mind attains ease, the body also finds ease."[33]

It struck me that my sleeplessness and recurring dreams were caused by my mental agitation, which in turn was caused by the unethical tasks Raja was assigning to me. I started to wonder about other psychosomatic disorders. It seemed to me that they were a common occurrence in the stressful work environments of my time.

"I understand the importance of maturing the mind," I said, after some thought. "Knowledge worker productivity can be improved with mind (*man*) maturity (agement). But how does this come about? What are some practical things I could do to make my mind more mature?"

"Woof!" barked the dog as he looked at the Yogi and then in the direction of a hut close to us.

"You have brought up a topic of great importance to Yogis," explained Yogi. "But first, you must be hungry."

The thought of food had not entered my mind. But suddenly I felt hungry.

"I know what you did," I said, laughing. "Or was it you?" I said, looking at the dog, which, I was beginning to realize, was not an ordinary dog.

"What did we do?" asked the Yogi, who was now smiling.

"The subtle is the cause, while the dense is the manifestation," I answered. "You planted the thought of food in my mind. And now my body is signaling hunger."

As soon as I said this, a Yogi in his twenties walked out of the hut. He was walking straight toward us. He greeted us with "Namaste" and spoke with Yogi in Sanskrit. He addressed Yogi as "Dharmaraja," or righteous king. My familiarity with Sanskrit was limited to the words in the Gita, so I could not understand clearly what the conversation was about. But I did understand that his name was Vaishampayana and that we were invited to join him for lunch. The timing of his arrival was incredible. He had definitely received a telepathic message from either Yogi or the dog. Vaishampayana left when Yogi nodded yes to his invitation.

"Vaishampayana is a student of Maharishi (great sage) Ved Vyasa," said Yogi. "The Maharishi has invited us to join his students and him for lunch. Let us proceed."

9. Yoga: The Art of Work

Lunch was being served outside the hut. As we got there, I saw around thirty students. It was a diverse group made up of both male and female students. Most of them must have been in their teens, though some were in their twenties. Their teacher came out of the hut and greeted Yogi and me. I was struck with amazement when I realized who it was. I was in the presence of the Maharishi Ved Vyasa, author of the Mahabharata and compiler of the Vedas, the most ancient Sanskrit scriptures. He had a long beard and hair, and was wearing several necklaces and bracelets made of *rudraksha* seeds.

We washed our hands and then took our seats. Yogi and I sat down next to the Maharishi. The students also took their seats. We were all sitting on simple mats of dried grass arranged in the form of a circle. Two students, who must have been assigned the responsibility for this lunch, brought out various items of food that had been cooked in copper pots. Each person took a serving from a pot and passed on the pot to the next person. One of the students responsible for the lunch took some food and served it to the dog before taking his seat.

We ate with our hands. For plates, we used the large leaves of a tree I could not recognize. The food was simple, vegetarian, and delicious. There was brown rice, which contained the bran and germ of rice, and was more nutritious than processed white rice. There were also a variety of lentils and vegetables cooked with delicious herbs and spices.

After lunch, Yogi spoke with the Maharishi for a few moments. As we were about to leave, the Maharishi materialized two objects in his palm which he then offered to me. One was a rosary (*mala*) and the other was a bracelet, both made of *rudraksha* seeds.

"*Rudraksha* beads, which the Maharishi has energized," explained Yogi.

The Maharishi also said, "*Jnana sethu.*" Yogi translated this phrase as "bridge of knowledge."

I thanked him and put on the gifts, with the bracelet on the wrist of my right hand. Yogi and I then took our leave and walked back toward the lake. At the lake, we paused to see the mountains, swans, and lotuses.

"The spiritual traditions of Bharat, the ancient South Asian subcontinent, were deep and intellectual," said Yogi. "Through mythology, ancient scholars preserved the essence of these traditions. It is for this reason you see concepts symbolized in the form of images, analogies, and characters in these mythological stories. In many instances, deep concepts were summarized into just one or a few verses, as was the case in the chariot and lamp/fire analogies we just discussed. In time you will uncover many such symbols.

"It is truly unfortunate that the colonizers of South Asia, due to immature minds and unawakened Intellects, did not look beneath these symbols. They saw only objects, from the perspective of wealth (*artha*) and pleasure (*kama*), but did not understand the symbolism in terms of righteousness (Dharma) and realization (*moksha*) of Atma. One cause of the prolonged global suffering of your time is because these colonizers took the material wealth, but not the true wealth, which are the spiritual traditions. Observe once again Padma, the lotus."

I looked at the lotus again. I remembered how it blooms in muddy waters and how water does not stick to its leaves.

"On the subject of the mind and five elements, we will look at one more analogy, summarized in verse 5.10 in the Gita," continued Yogi.

He who does actions forsaking attachment, resigning them to Brahman, is not soiled by evil, like unto a lotus-leaf by water.
—Lord Krishna in the Bhagavad Gita, 5.10

"You have already seen how water freely flows off the lotus leaf," continued Yogi. "The lotus has another special quality. Different parts of the plant are associated with each of the five elements. The roots are firmly attached with the earth at the bottom of the lake. The stem resides in water. The leaf is energized by the rays of the sun, a very large mass of fire. The petals bloom in the air. And all parts of the lotus have space within them, just as all material objects have space inside them. Now link these lotus parts to the human body, by means of the five elements."

"The roots, via earth, would be linked to the physical body," I replied. "The stem, via water, would be linked to the senses. The leaf, via fire, would be linked to the mind. And the petals, via air, would be linked to the Intellect."

"Then, based on the verse, what does the lotus symbolize?"

I took a few moments to think this over.

"The lotus is a symbol of purity," I replied. "It blooms in muddy waters, which are clean in some parts and dirty in others. But it does not let the water stick to its leaves. Humans also live in a world that contains purity as well as toxicity. The five ordinary senses are constantly bombarded by this purity and toxicity. But the mind must remain unattached to these inputs coming from the senses, as the lotus leaf lets water flow off it freely."

Once again, to help me remember these concepts, I arranged them in the form of a table.

Vibratory Element	Sheath of Body	Lotus Analogy
Space (*Akasha*)	Bliss sheath	Entire plant
Air	Intellect (*buddhi*)	Petals
Fire	Mind (*man*)	Leaf
Water	Senses	Stem
Earth	Physical body	Roots

"The lotus leaf symbolizes the concept of Non-attachment (*tyaga*)." Yogi explained further. "You asked for practical ways to make the mind more mature. Keeping yourself non-attached to rewards or results of actions is a powerful practice that matures the mind."

"But the business world is focused on results." I tried to show Yogi what I meant by writing a simple equation on the paper:

Knowledge + Action = Results

"Do you see what I mean?" I asked Yogi. "Drucker describes it this way:

"The knowledge we now consider knowledge proves itself in action. **What we now mean by knowledge is information effective in action, information focused on results.** The results are seen outside the person – in society and economy, or in the advancement of knowledge itself."[34]
—Peter Drucker

Yogi smiled at me. "These ideas are largely compatible with the Yoga-Vedanta philosophy I am teaching you. Review the verses 3.3, 2.47, 2.48, and 3.25 from the Gita and relate them to this equation."

In the beginning (of creation), O sinless one, the twofold path of devotion was given by Me to this world;—the path of knowledge (*jnana*) for the meditative, the path of work (karma) for the active.
—Lord Krishna in the Bhagavad Gita, 3.3

Thy right is to work (karma) only; but never to the fruits thereof. Be thou not the producer of the fruits of (thy) actions; neither let thy attachment be towards inaction.
Being steadfast in Yoga, Dhananjaya [Prince Arjuna], perform actions, abandoning attachment, remaining unconcerned as regards success and

failure. This *samatvam* [evenness, balance] of mind (in regard to success and failure) is known as Yoga.
—Lord Krishna in the Bhagavad Gita, 2.47, 48

As do the unwise, attached to work, act, so should the wise act, O descendant of Bharata [Prince Arjuna], (but) without attachment, desirous of the guidance of the world.
—Lord Krishna in the Bhagavad Gita, 3.25

The first verse is about the path of knowledge (*jnana*) and the path of action/work (karma). The second verse explains that one must do work for the sake of the work, but not for the fruits (results or rewards) of the work. The third verse explains that one must perform work by being non-attached to the results of work, whether they result in success or failure. It also defines Yoga as an evenness or balance of mind. The fourth verse is also about non-attachment.

"I still don't understand," I said to Yogi. "How can I analyze scenarios and recommend options to clients while remaining non-attached to the outcomes of these scenarios?"

"To answer that question, we must start with the four classical Yogas that make up the practice of Yoga. As you may recall, Swami Vivekenanda covered these in the lectures I brought you to."

1. The Yoga of Action (Karma-Yoga)
2. The Yoga of Knowledge (Jnana-Yoga)
3. The Yoga of Meditation (Raja-Yoga)
4. The Yoga of Devotion (Bhakti-Yoga)

"Yes, I remember now."

"Good. Knowledge (*jnana*), action/work (karma) and results, referred to as *karma-phala* (fruits of action/work) are core concepts in the Gita. Do you recall how Swami Vivekananda explained Karma-Yoga?"

I relaxed my mind and looked through my third eye. I could see Swami Vivekenanda standing at his podium, and I let his words wash over me again:

"The word Karma is derived from the Sanskrit *Kri*, to do; all action is Karma. Technically, this word also means the effects of actions. In connection with metaphysics, it sometimes means the effects, of which our past actions were the causes. But in Karma-Yoga we have simply to do with the word Karma as meaning work."
—Swami Vivekananda[35]

I opened my eyes and saw Yogi looking at me. "Keep listening," he said.

"The Swami has more to tell you."

I closed my eyes again and mentally returned to the lecture.

"Work for work's sake. There are some who are really the salt of the earth in every country and who work for work's sake, who do not care for name, or fame, or even to go to heaven. They work just because good will come of it."

—Swami Vivekananda[36]

"Yogi, I derived the equation on knowledge, action, and results from Management philosophies, but I am starting to see the ways that the philosophies of Yoga-Vedanta can be linked to it. However, there is one simple yet significant difference. Look." I crossed out my original equation and replaced it with a revised version:

Knowledge Work Equation:

Knowledge (*jnana*) + Action (*karma*) = Results (*karma-phala*)

K + A = R

"The essential difference between Management and Yoga-Vedanta is in which side of the Knowledge Work Equation the focus is on. Management is 'focused on results,' i.e., the right-hand side or RHS of the equation. In Yoga-Vedanta, the focus is on the left-hand side or LHS of the equation, i.e., on doing the work while remaining non-attached to the results (fruits) of the work. In Management, the focus is often on results that 'are seen outside the person—in society and economy, or in the advancement of knowledge itself.'[37] In Yoga-Vedanta, the focus is on the worker's knowledge and action, on her or his contribution through work rather than on the results obtained from work."

I explained these thoughts to Yogi, who acknowledged that I was on the right track.

"Non-attachment can be applied to any kind of work," replied Yogi. "Also to the task the Maharishi gave you."

"What task?" I asked. "He did not say anything to me."

"He did."

I remembered the words knowledge (*jnana*) and bridge (*sethu*).

"He wanted me to build a bridge of knowledge?" I said.

Yogi nodded in agreement.

"A bridge between what and what?" I asked.

"The world that you came from and the world that you are experiencing right now," replied Yogi.

"I come from the material world of business. I am experiencing the spiritual world of yogis. I am to bridge business and spirituality?"

"Yes. But your task is more specific."

"I am to bridge Management with Yoga-Vedanta."

Yogi smiled and nodded. Thoughts and doubts raced through my mind.

"I am not qualified for this task," I replied. "I wouldn't know where to start. Maybe I could write a book." I looked down at the stack of papers in my hands, the frameworks I had sketched out and the principles I had written down. I had never imagined writing a book before, but now I believed that I could do it. I suddenly felt joyful and charged with purpose. But then, just as suddenly, I felt my doubts and anxieties set in again.

"But what if I put in a lot of work and wrote a book and it is never published? What if it is published, but is not a success? What if after all my work the book does not sell enough copies and fails to make a difference? What if I draw severe criticism from experts and critics and look like a fool?"

"Remain non-attached to results," advised Yogi. "Focus on knowledge and action, your contributions through your work rather than the results obtained from your work. Consider your motive (the why) and the means (the how) for doing the work."

I considered this in terms of the Knowledge Work Equation. The publication of my book as well as the success of the publication are 'results of work' and fall on the RHS of the equation. Each time doubts entered my mind, I needed to remind myself that my focus should be on the LHS of the equation. Some doubts remained.

"I understand the philosophical reasons of non-attachment to results," I said. "Work done with non-attachment to results would be work done for Dharma—righteousness and duty. Is there also a practical aspect to non-attachment to results?"

"What was your state of mind when you realized your task?" asked Yogi.

"I was worried and doubtful."

"You were thinking about future events. You were focusing on the fruits of your work, future rewards, and results of your actions. Your mind was not focused on the task assigned to you. You were wasting your energy worrying about the future, which is dependent on multiple events and factors, not all of which are under your influence. By concentrating on the work, your mind is focused on what you can influence, on your contributions, knowledge, and actions. You will be more productive. And by not worrying about results, you will not have doubts and distractions."

I paused and thought about Yogi's explanations. I began to understand both the philosophical and practical reasons for non-attachment to results. But another doubt entered my mind.

"I understand your point regarding focusing on what we can influence,"

I said. "But would we be leaving too much to fate and destiny?"

"Weak-minded persons regard destiny as supreme and unavoidable,"[38] answered Yogi, as he quoted multiple sections of the Mahabharata. "Everything in the world depends on destiny and exertion. But destiny can never be successful except by timely exertion.[39] In all acts, the attainment of success is always uncertain. Knowing that success is uncertain, people still act, so that they sometimes succeed and sometimes do not. However, those who abstain from action never obtain success. In the absence of exertion, there is but one result—the absence of success. However, there are two possible results in the case of exertion—the acquisition of success or its non-acquisition.[40] An intelligent person who has applied proper means should not grieve if a purpose pursued does not succeed."[41]

"You make valid points," I replied. "But failure leads to unhappiness and it is difficult not to grieve when one has failed."

"One who has never been afflicted with calamity can never have prosperity,"[42] was Yogi's response. "People experience happiness and misery by turns, for no person ever enjoyed continuous happiness. A wise person endowed with high wisdom, knowing that life has its ups and downs, is neither filled with joy nor with grief. When happiness comes, one should enjoy it. When misery comes, one should bear it."[43]

This time I nodded in agreement.

"What will you call your bridge between Management and Yoga-Vedanta?" asked Yogi.

"Both Management and Yoga are practices," I answered, after some thought. "Vedanta deals with philosophical aspects. For the sake of simplicity, I will combine the names of the two practices and call the bridge Yogic Management."

After giving a name to my "bridge of knowledge," another thought entered my mind.

"It will be difficult to translate the idea of non-attachment in a business context," I said. "I think many people will confuse non-attachment to results with non-attachment to work itself. This may lead to people renouncing work altogether. Or it may lead to indifference, an attitude where people do not care about the work."

"Some may find non-attachment confusing," responded Yogi. "But the Gita can help you explain the idea. The Gita clearly states the difference between *tyaga*, the non-attachment to fruits of work, and *sannyasa*, the renunciation of all actions that are motivated by desires. The Gita also clearly states that action is superior to inaction. If someone who claims to be practicing the Gita's teachings is lazy and inactive, understand that his or her lack of action is caused by ignorance."

Relevant verses from the Gita entered my mind.

The renunciation of *Kamya* [motivated by desire] actions, the sages understand as *Sannyasa*: the wise declare the abandonment of the fruits of all works as *Tyaga*.
—Lord Krishna in the Bhagavad Gita, 18.2

By non-performance of work none reaches worklessness; by merely giving up action no one attains to perfection.
—Lord Krishna in the Bhagavad Gita, 3.4

Do thou perform obligatory action; for action is superior to inaction, and even the bare maintenance of thy body would not be possible if thou art inactive.
—Lord Krishna in the Bhagavad Gita, 3.8

"You must do work because it is your duty to do it," continued Yogi. "To not discharge one's duties is idleness.[44] Understand that *tyaga* is renunciation of the fruits of work or the non-attachment to fruits of work. It is not the renunciation of work altogether. Also understand that it does not mean indifference. One must care about the work and about the results of work. The point to be mindful of is that this work must be performed while remaining non-attached to the results (fruits) of the work. With practice, you will realize something amazing. **The most rewarding work is that which is done for the work and not for the rewards.** Do you now understand the principle of non-attachment to fruits?"

"Yes," I replied after reviewing these verses and Yogi's explanations.

"Good. Then let's build upon your understanding of Karma-Yoga," continued Yogi. "In Karma-Yoga, what work is done is less important than why and how it is done. There are three things that a yogi should take into consideration while performing work. These are the motive, the state of mind, and the means utilized to do the work. Using the Intellect, one must make decisions with a pure motive, always taking into consideration Dharma (righteousness, duty). One should then perform actions using a mature mind and by using proper means. You could link motive, mind, and means to three of the five elements—air (symbolized as a circle), fire (symbolized as a triangle), and water (symbolized as a crescent). This follows the principle that the subtle leads to the dense. Here the mind, like fire, is a medium of illumination through which the Atma's luminescence is radiated."

"Yogi, the concept of the mature and illuminating mind sounds very similar to the 'positive' mind that many self-improvement authors have written about. Let me see if I can put these ideas together to form a framework." I took out a new sheet of paper and began to draw.

Motive-Mind-Means Framework

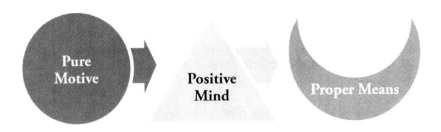

A Yogic Manager practicing Karma-Yoga makes decisions with a pure motive and then performs action with a positive mind and by using proper means. A Yogic Manager works for the sake of Dharma (righteousness, duty) while remaining non-attached to the results (fruits) of work. Before performing any work, three questions need to be answered:

1.   Are my decisions based on pure motives?
2.   Am I performing work with a positive mind?
3.   Am I using proper means?

I looked at the framework I had just developed and thought about how it might be able to help me resolve my crisis regarding Option 4:

1.   **Are my decisions based on pure motives?**

No. My reasons were selfish. I was motivated by my promotion and higher salary, and by my debt to Raja, who had helped me tremendously.

2.   **Am I performing work with a positive mind?**

No. My mind was clouded by my desire for wealth and success. A mature mind would have factored in righteousness in addition to results.

3.   **Am I using proper means?**

No. I was using deception to unnecessarily complicate advice that could be presented more clearly. My slides highlighted the profitability of Option 4, but did not go through the known risks. Clearly, there are health and environmental risks to the villagers and wildlife in this option. But there are also reputational risks and possible legal ramifications, which our clients should be advised to take into consideration.

I had three questions with "no" for an answer. Clearly, Option 4 needed to be reconsidered.

"Yogi, what if behaving ethically means that you will displease a client, lose a contract, lose a promotion, or get fired? I mean, non-attachment to results and focusing on work are powerful principles, but what about success? What you are talking about requires a paradigm shift in my thinking. I have always been in the pursuit of success. I find it hard to have evenness of mind with regard to success and failure."

"Do you want guaranteed success?" asked Yogi.

"Guaranteed success is no light claim. Did you really just say 'guaranteed' success?"

"Yes. It is possible for a person to <u>always</u> be successful. Do you want to learn how?"

"Yes," I replied, eagerly waiting for the answer.

I could not believe my ears. Thousands of books have been published and continue to be published that fall under the self-improvement or "success" genre. The authors provide a variety of tools and techniques intended to make the reader successful. They contain "secrets" and "keys," and provide instructions for great achievements. I had read a few books in this genre and had found them quite beneficial in making my thinking more positive. However, I had never read a book that included a claim of guaranteed success.

"For guaranteed success, you must understand two definitions of Yoga," continued Yogi. "Review verse 2.48 again, along with the two verses after it."

Being steadfast in Yoga, Dhananjaya [Prince Arjuna], perform actions, abandoning attachment, remaining unconcerned as regards success and failure. This *samatvam* [evenness, balance] of mind (in regard to success and failure) is known as Yoga. [2.48]

Work (with desire) is verily far inferior to that performed with the mind undisturbed by thoughts of results. O Dhananjaya, seek refuge in this evenness of mind. Wretched are they who act for results. [2.49]

Endued with this evenness of mind, one frees oneself in this life, alike from vice and virtue. Devote thyself, therefore, to this Yoga. Yoga is the very *kausalam* [art, skill] of work. [2.50]

—Lord Krishna in the Bhagavad Gita, 2.48 to 50

"In these verses, there are two definitions of Yoga," explained Yogi. "The first is in *samatvam*, verse 2.48: **Yoga is evenness or balance of mind**. The second is in *kausalam*, verse 2.50: **Yoga is the art of work**, or Yoga is skill in action. Notice that **Yoga is an end as well as the means to the end**. It is both the destination and the journey."

I suddenly remembered Swami Vivekananda explaining the secret of work in one of his lectures. It had come from a conversation he had with a great Yogi in India:

"He told me once the secret of work, **'Let the end and the means be joined into one.'** When you are doing any work, do not think of anything beyond. Do it as worship, as the highest worship, and devote your whole life to it for the time being."
—Swami Vivekananda[45]

Do you now understand how to get guaranteed success?" asked Yogi.

I paused to absorb these ideas. I had been trained to think that work is war and had heard Raja quote repeatedly from *The Art of War*. Now I was being advised to think of work as worship and to practice Yoga, the art of work. This required a significant change in my way of thinking.

"Yes," I replied after some thought. "**Guaranteed success is possible if the work is the ends as well as the means. Karma-Yoga is a practice that can guarantee success for the practitioner. By focusing on the work while remaining non-attached to the results and by letting the ends and the means being joined into one, the Karma-yogi is always successful.** But the success you are talking about is spiritual, rather than financial. I find it difficult to think of success that cannot be measured and is not related to wealth."

"It is not a balanced approach to think of success only in terms of wealth," replied Yogi. "Such thinking gives people the incentive to be greedy and to strive for success by any means necessary, without taking into consideration society and the Earth, of which they are a part. Holistic thinking that takes into consideration righteousness, wealth, pleasure, and realization will benefit the individual as well as society and all living beings."

"You have a good point, Yogi, but I am still finding it difficult to think of success in holistic terms."

"Sometimes, a concept cannot be integrated into consciousness right away," said Yogi. "Sometimes you need to meditate on an idea. The mantra you are developing should help you with this. Can you summarize some of the ideas we just discussed and add new lines to the mantra?"

I thought about it for a minute. Then I pulled out the page with the beginnings of my mantra on it and wrote:

From performing work as war, lead me to performing work as worship,
From practicing the art of war, lead me to practicing Yoga, the art of work.

"Good," Yogi smiled.

I looked back down at the page and decided to add a title. I wrote "Yogic Management Mantra" at the top.

"When you meditate," said Yogi, "You are trying to achieve the

Supreme State. This description of Yoga comes from the Upanishads, which predate the Gita."

> When the five instruments of knowledge [i.e. senses] stand still, together with the mind (*man*) and when the Intellect (*buddhi*) does not move, that is called the Supreme State.
> This, the firm control of the senses, is what is called yoga. One must then be vigilant; for yoga can be both beneficial and injurious.
> —Katha Upanishad, 2.3.10 & 2.3.11

Yogi was about to explain further when I interrupted him.

"Wait a minute. How can Yoga be both beneficial and injurious?"

"If practiced correctly, Yoga can be very beneficial," answered Yogi. "It can lead to tremendous physical, intellectual, and spiritual advancement. However, if Yoga is practiced incorrectly, one can harm oneself. If an action is done wrongly it can lead to physical injury. If a concept is inaccurately interpreted, it could negate intellectual growth. If the energy produced during the rise in consciousness is channeled incorrectly, it can lead to spiritual injuries and, in extreme cases, insanity. For this reason, a student should always get trained by qualified teachers."

The thought of Raja as a teacher entered my mind. Was he a qualified teacher? Was he misapplying the concepts of *The Art of War* and other books for his own personal gain?

"We have discussed many Karma-Yoga concepts," I said. "I am trying to relate these concepts to two factors that are important to managers. How do these concepts relate to effectiveness and efficiency?"

"What do these terms mean to you?" asked Yogi.

I quoted Drucker once again:

> "Efficiency is doing things right; effectiveness is doing the right things."
> —Peter Drucker

"And how do these terms and definitions relate to the equation you sketched out earlier?"

I looked down at the equation:

Knowledge + Action = Results

"Efficiency relates to the performance of actions," I stated, after thinking for a few moments. "Success, in terms of efficiency and doing things right, is dependent upon the results of the work. If the actual results of a task met or exceeded the requirements planned for the task, the task is judged to be successful, or having been done right. If the planned requirements are not delivered, the task is considered to be a failure. In contrast, effectiveness is driven by motives. These are related to knowledge. Success in terms of effectiveness, doing the right things, is also dependent upon the results of the work. A manager may determine that the right thing to do is to grow shareholder value, which may be at the expense of the environment as per the limits currently outlined by the law. This may be legal but may not necessarily be righteous or ethical. For effectiveness, as well as for efficiency, success and failure are dependent upon the results, or the RHS of the Knowledge Work Equation. In management, the manager is advised to be effective and efficient. It follows that an effective and efficient manager needs to do the right things right."

"Now, think as a Karma-yogi," suggested Yogi.

"A manager practicing Karma-Yoga must not only be effective and efficient, but must also go a step further," I replied. "Such a manager must apply knowledge for results and apply wisdom, the subset of knowledge that is applied for righteousness (Dharma). Applying the Motive-Mind-Means Framework, a Yogic Manager practicing Karma-Yoga makes decisions with a pure motive, and then performs action with a positive mind and by using proper means, for the sake of Dharma while remaining non-attached to the results (fruits) of the work. The motive is doing the righteous thing. Actions are performed using righteous means. Hence, the Yogic Manager needs to do the righteous thing righteously. The focus is on the LHS of the Knowledge Work Equation."

I summarized and explained this thought to Yogi.

An effective and efficient manager does the right things right. A Yogic Manager practicing Karma-Yoga does the righteous thing righteously.

I added another line to the Yogic Management Mantra.

From doing the right things right, lead me to do the righteous thing righteously.

Option 4 took into consideration results but did not factor in righteousness. If I practiced Yogic Management, I could not present this option to the client. A yogic manager would present the option that is the most profitable within the bounds of righteousness and ethics.

This was easy enough to say, but how would I feel once I was standing in front of Raja, knowing that my decision would incur his disappointment? I needed to understand more about Yogi's philosophy before I could determine what option to present.

I summarized the recent concepts into principles. Since I had started thinking of the bridge I was building as Yogic Management, I decided that these principles should be called the Principles of Yogic Management.

Achieve guaranteed success by performing work for the sake of the work and not for the results of the work. Let the ends and the means be joined as one by treating your work as the ends as well as the means to the end.

Practicing non-attachment to the fruits (results) of work, focus on what you can influence, on your contributions, knowledge, and actions. Do not get distracted and waste your energy worrying about future outcomes that are not completely under your influence.

Make decisions with a pure motive and then perform actions with a positive mind and by using proper means.

"Let's also review *samatvam* Yoga, the description of Yoga as evenness or balance," continued Yogi, after I had compiled the principles. "These contain further practical suggestions for maintaining evenness. Review the Gita verses 6.16 and 6.17."

(Success in) Yoga is not for him who eats too much or too little - nor, O Arjuna, for him who sleeps too much or too little.
To him who is temperate in eating and recreation, in his effort for work, and in sleep and wakefulness, Yoga becomes the destroyer of misery.
—Lord Krishna in the Bhagavad Gita, 6.16, 17

"A simple concept," I replied.
"True," added Yogi. "Simple but important, and easily forgotten."
"I often have difficulty sleeping."
"Balance your mind with Yoga and meditation. Once you have done that, you will sleep better."
Yoga as balance or evenness led to the next principle:

Live a balanced lifestyle by being balanced in work, relaxation, recreation, and all other activities.

"Many Yoga-Vedanta concepts are simple to understand," continued Yogi. "Yet, in practice, they can be applied in a variety of ways. *Samatvam* (evenness, balance) also applies to how one treats others. Review the Gita verse 6.9."

He attains excellence who looks with equal regard upon well-wishers, friends, foes, neutrals, arbiters, the hateful, the relatives, and upon the righteous and the unrighteous alike.
—Lord Krishna in the Bhagavad Gita, 6.9

"How would you apply this verse to your work?" asked Yogi.

I took a few moments to review this verse in the context of the workplace. Many thoughts entered my mind. I remembered my role in firing the fifteen people who had joined Characterra from Singh and Patel Consulting. If I had reviewed Raja's list with more alertness, I would have discerned that age discrimination was involved.

"Always treat people equally," I replied. "Never discriminate against anybody based on their gender, race, ethnicity, religion, age, or any other criteria. In all managerial activities (the assignment of roles, selection of successors, rewarding or promoting employees, etc.), make decisions based upon the contributions, knowledge, and skills of employees. Never be partial because an employee is a friend or a relative."

These thoughts led to the next principle.

Always treat people equally. Never discriminate against anybody based on their gender, race, ethnicity, religion, age, or any other criteria.

10. The Splendor of a Thousand Suns

"Yoga as the art of work and as evenness or balance of mind is indeed an inspiring point of view," I said to Yogi after much thought. "However, this idea is difficult to implement because the mind is restless and behaves in ways it is used to behaving in. I am finding it difficult to focus my mind and change my way of thinking. When one has been thinking in a particular way for several years, it becomes difficult to change that way of thinking. I know that I am struggling with this as I listen to you explain these philosophical concepts. My mind is drawn toward success, competition, winning, and other war-like tendencies. I find it a challenge to progress from the art of war to the art of work. I am starting to wonder if implementing yogic principles requires a much stronger character than I possess."

"Your words echo the words of Prince Arjuna, who also expressed doubts about the teaching of the Gita," replied Yogi. "In reply, Lord Krishna advised him to govern his mind through the next principle we will discuss: practice. Through practice, one's character can be built."

The verse Yogi was hinting at entered my mind.

Without doubt, O mighty-armed, the mind is restless, and difficult to control; but through practice and renunciation, O son of Kunti, it may be governed.
—Lord Krishna in the Bhagavad Gita, 6.35

"Link practice to Swami Vivekananda's speech on character," continued Yogi. "In one of his lectures he talked about *samskaras*, which he translated as 'inherent tendencies.' He explained how every action a person performs, in thought, word, or deed, leaves an impression on the person's mind. These impressions influence a person to behave in certain ways."

I recalled the Swami's speech that Yogi was referring to.

"Every work that we do, every movement of the body, every thought that we think, leaves such an impression on the mind-stuff, and even when such impressions are not obvious on the surface, they are sufficiently strong to work beneath the surface, subconsciously. ...
If a man continuously hears bad words, thinks bad thoughts, does bad actions, his mind will be full of bad impressions; and they will influence his thought and work without his being conscious of the fact. ...

Similarly, if a man thinks good thoughts and does good works, the sum total of these impressions will be good; and they, in a similar manner, will force him to do good even in spite of himself. When a man has done so much good work and thought so many good thoughts that there is an irresistible tendency in him to do good, in spite of himself and even if he wishes to do evil, his mind, as the sum total of his tendencies, will not allow him to do so; the tendencies will turn him back; he is completely under the influence of the good tendencies. When such is the case, a man's good character is said to be established."
—Swami Vivekananda[46]

"Karma (work, action) can be in the form of thought, word, or deed," continued Yogi. "As discussed, the subtle is the cause and the dense is the manifestation. Thoughts, which are the subtlest of the three, can lead to words spoken or written and to deeds performed. Words, the next in terms of subtlety, can also lead to deeds. If you keep practicing good thoughts, words, and deeds, you can establish a strong and good character. So, whenever you get a chance, fill your mind with thoughts that are illuminating, pure, and righteous. Over time, and with practice, you will alter your way of thinking and build your character."

"This makes sense from a scientific perspective, as well," I told Yogi, remembering the biology classes I had taken. "Neurons and synapses in the brain process and transmit information through electrical or chemical signals. Cells that are stimulated can strengthen by forming additional connections. Cells and connections that are not used can weaken and die. So, in a very real way, thoughts can alter one's brain and mold one's character."

"Yes," replied Yogi. "This can be done through practice and over time. A good time to fill your mind with positive, pure, and righteous thoughts is in the morning, soon after your daily cleansing activities. Many righteous persons have built their characters by reading texts like the Upanishads and Bhagavad Gita in the morning. If you do so, you may start to notice that your entire day goes better than the days when you do not fill your mind with beneficial thoughts.

"Remember that repeatedly perpetrating unrighteous acts destroys intelligence. And the person who has lost intelligence repeatedly commits unrighteous acts. Dharma, repeatedly practiced, enhances intelligence. And the person whose intelligence has increased repeatedly practices Dharma.[47] One's character is built and strengthened as this process is repeated."

I thought of Peter Drucker. "So, the most important criteria to hiring a person should be her or his character?"

"Yes. A good office is never wasted if it is assigned to the good and righteous."[48]

I felt a painful twinge as I remembered the fifteen employees I had let go. Professor Pi had a good and righteous character, as did the others.

I summarized the ideas Yogi was sharing and added them to my growing list of Yogic Management principles:

Fill your mind with positive, pure, and righteous thoughts, which you put into practice in words, spoken or written, and in deeds performed. Establish your character by always practicing good thoughts, words, and deeds.

Make character the most important criteria you use when you hire employees. A position is never wasted if it is assigned to the good and righteous.

"I have read many books on success and self-improvement," I said, after my moments of silence and contemplation. "I'd like to hear your thoughts on the connection between the mind and success. Some people say that if you truly want something with all your mind, the universe will give it to you. Some call this a universal 'secret' or 'law.' What do you think?"

"The statement is inaccurate," replied Yogi. The principle that you are referring to relates not to the mind but to the Atma. It is not just about thought, but about thought done in a meditative or yogic state. The mind and Intellect need to be absorbed in the Atma for this to work. When these three are in harmony, the object of meditation becomes manifested.

This was another shift in thinking for me. I realized that in order to accomplish goals, mere thought was insufficient. One must, through Yoga and meditation, merge the mind with the Intellect and merge the Intellect with the Atma.

"The mind is indeed a powerful instrument," continued Yogi. "But the Atma is greater than the mind. The light of the One is within you."

"The power of the One is within me?" I said in amazement.

"Correct," replied Yogi. "Review verse 5.24 from the Gita."

Whose happiness is within, whose relaxation is within, whose light is within, that Yogi alone, becoming Brahman, gains absolute freedom.
—Lord Krishna in the Bhagavad Gita, 5.24

"On several occasions I have derived strength from external factors," I replied. "My manager, Raja, has often praised and motivated me to drive myself further."

"A Yogi does not require words of praise or motivation. What would happen if your manager gave you neither?"

"My growth and achievements would be limited. You're right that my performance should never depend on such external factors. But what about competition? I have often compared myself to my peers and motivated myself to do better than them."

"What did Swami Vivekananda say about competition?"

I remembered the Swami's words.

"Competition rouses envy, and it kills the kindliness of the heart."
—Swami Vivekananda[49]

"Like the lotus, you must be a source of purity, not toxicity," advised Yogi. "There is enough toxicity on Earth. Don't add to the toxicity by being a source of competition and envy at your work. Also, what happens if you compete with mediocre peers?"

"Being better than them would be easy," I replied. "Again, I would be limiting myself to external factors. I would rise only to the levels of my peers. However, if I work to the best of my abilities and meditate on the Atma, I will rise to my true potential for greatness."

"The principle applies to all external factors," added Yogi. "The power of the One is within you. Derive your strength, light, energy, and motivation from your Atma."

I summarized these teachings into a principle.

Derive strength from your Atma, the source of tremendous light and energy that resides within your body's five sheaths. Don't limit your potential for greatness by relying on praise or competition from external sources for your motivation.

"This principle applies only to yogis," continued Yogi. "Be mindful that many of the people you work with are not yogis. Although you don't require external motivation, they might. You must continue to motivate them so they may make themselves better."

I nodded in agreement.

"We have spoken about the light within," continued Yogi. "But the Gita verse, 5.24, that we just discussed also mentioned happiness and relaxation within. Through Yoga, you can get both happiness and relaxation within."

11. The Purposeful Life

"There comes a point in most people's lives when they start to ask deep and difficult to answer questions," I said. "I have asked myself one question in particular several times over the last few years. What is the purpose of life?"

Yogi paused for a few moments before responding. Two students walked passed us tending around a dozen or so cows. They greeted us and we returned their greetings.

"We have already discussed the four values: Dharma, wealth, pleasure, and the realization of Atma," said Yogi, after the students left. "I will now explain another concept that will help you decide for yourself what you want your life's purpose to be."

"Please explain the concept."

"The ancient practitioners of Dharma considered human life to be made up of four phases or houses (*ashramas*). These four, in order, are:

1.   Student Phase (*Brahmacharya*)
2.   Householder Phase (*Grihastha*)
3.   Retiree Phase (*Vanaprastha*)
4.   Renunciation Phase (*Sannyasa*)

"In all four phases, the person should be focused on practicing the value of Dharma (righteousness, duty). In the student phase, the person is primarily concerned with Dharma. In the householder phase, the person is to pursue wealth and is entitled to the enjoyment of pleasure, in addition to practicing Dharma. The retiree phase is a transitional phase in which the person prepares for the final phase. The retiree acts as a mentor to the next generation by passing on wealth and information for the betterment of society. The retiree phase, *vanaprastha*, gets its name from forest (*vana*). The forest was a place of great learning in ancient times and had many schools, such as the ones you see around you. In the final phase, the renunciation phase, the person must detach from the world and focus on the realization of Atma."

I thought about how I could represent the concepts Yogi had explained in a way that would match the life phases of the modern world. I translated the student, householder, retiree, and renunciation phases into:

1. Student Phase
2. Professional Phase
3. Philanthropist Phase
4. Spiritualist Phase

At this point in my life, I had completed the student phase and was in the professional phase. My colleagues at Characterra, including Raja, were also in the professional phases of their lives.

I suddenly remembered a famous quote which I repeated to Yogi.

"Find purpose, the means will follow."
—Mahatma Gandhi

"Yes, that is an insightful approach," said Yogi. "But both purpose and means are so interconnected that it is sometimes hard to see which one comes first. One's purposes depend on means for their success. Means are dependent upon the nature of the purposes sought to be accomplished by them. They are intimately connected with each other, so much so that success depends on both."[50]

"We discussed similar concepts in relation to the Motive-Mind-Means Framework," I replied. "Pure motive, positive mind, and proper means. Purpose and motive are linked. I will think of the four phases in terms of motives and means."

"For now, let's focus on motives. What does the Bhagavad Gita say about the ego (ahamkara)?" asked Yogi.

Some relevant verses entered my mind.

Earth, water, fire, air, space, mind [man], Intellect [buddhi], and egoism [ahamkara]: thus is My Prakriti [Nature, matter] divided eight-fold.
—Lord Krishna in the Bhagavad Gita, 7.4

"So, ego is different from the Intellect?"

"Yes. The ego, like the Intellect, is a subset of the mind. However, the Intellect may be focused on either the Atma or the ego. What does the Gita say about people who focus on the Atma rather than the ego?"

More relevant verses entered my mind.

He who hates no creature, and is friendly and compassionate towards all, who is free from the feelings of 'I and mine' [ahamkara], even-minded in pain and pleasure, forbearing, ever content, steady in meditation, self-controlled, and possessed of firm conviction, with mind and Intellect fixed on Me—he who is thus devoted to Me, is dear to Me.
—Lord Krishna in the Bhagavad Gita, 12.13, 14

Forsaking egoism [*ahamkara*], power, pride, lust, wrath and property, freed from the notion of "mine," and tranquil, he is fit for becoming Brahman.
—Lord Krishna in the Bhagavad Gita, 18.53

"Good," smiled Yogi. "And what does the Gita say about people who focus on the ego?"

Possessed of egoism [*ahamkara*], power, insolence, lust and wrath, these malignant people hate Me (the Self within) in their own bodies and those of others.
—Lord Krishna in the Bhagavad Gita, 16.18

As I thought of these verses, I realized that the ego played a larger role for students and professionals in the first two phases of life, during the acquisition of knowledge and wealth. In terms of the Reality-Consciousness-Bliss Framework, an egoistic person would be at the stage of individual consciousness, at about 3.0 out of 5.0 on the scale of consciousness.

The transition between the student phase and the professional phase is quite simple to understand. Students become professionals when they finish their studies and become working professionals. While they were students, society invested in their education. As professionals, they take a more active role in society by participating in sectors such as the business, government, or nonprofit sectors. However, the transition between the professional phase and the philanthropist phase is not as obvious.

"In the student and the professional phases, the emphasis tends to be on the individual," I said to Yogi. "I would say that the motives in these phases could be categorized as ego gratification. But there comes a point when the consciousness of the professional expands beyond the individual to include others—maybe the entire Earth or the entire universe. This transformation takes the human from the professional phase to the philanthropist phase, in the process transforming work into service. The motive changes in the last two phases from the gratification of the ego (*ahamkara*, false self) to the realization of the Atma (soul, true Self). What is the turning point in human consciousness between the professional and philanthropist phases?"

"You have made important observations," replied Yogi. "We will talk about the turning point soon. First, however, we must turn from motives to means. I will introduce you next to the term education (*vidya*) with verses taken from a Sanskrit text called the Hitopadesa."

The wise should pursue education (*vidya*) and wealth (*artha*) as if they
were to live forever;
They should practice Dharma as if they were to die at any moment.
—Hitopadesa, Prologue, Verse 3

True education (*vidya*) teaches humility, from which one builds
character;
From character one obtains wealth, which leads to the establishment of
Dharma, which leads to happiness.
—Hitopadesa, Prologue, Verse 6

The first verse had striking similarities with another famous quote from
Mahatma Gandhi: "Live as if you were to die tomorrow. Learn as if you
were to live forever." The second verse was an amazingly concise summary
of the key concepts I had been discussing with Yogi.

"Education is also dealt with in the Upanishads," continued Yogi, who
then recited three more verses.

Into a blind darkness enter those who engage in *avidya* (work) alone; but
into a greater darkness they enter who engage in *vidya* (education) alone.
One thing, they say, is obtained from *vidya* (education); another, they say,
from *avidya* (work). Thus we have heard from the wise who have taught
us this.
One who is aware that both *vidya* (education) and *avidya* (work) should
be pursued together, overcomes death through *avidya* (work) and obtains
immortality through *vidya* (education).
—Isa Upanishad, 9 to 11

"Yogi, I can't help recalling our conversation about *jnana* and *ajnana*.
Jnana was knowledge, and *ajnana* was ignorance, the opposite of knowledge.
Dharma was righteousness, and *adharma* was unrighteousness. Does this
mean that work (*avidya*) is the negative opposite of education (*vidya*)?"
"Review the verses again, Arjun, and you will see that they do not
suggest that education can replace work or be conducted to the exclusion of
work, the way that *jnana* opposes *ajnana*. The verses recommend a balance
between theory and practice, or between knowledge and action. In this
context, *avidya* can be thought of as a synonym of karma (work, action)."
"I see. So the means for moving through each of the four life phases is
education as well as work," I replied. "In the student phase, the means of
advancement would be education. In the professional phase, wealth is
generated by the means of work. In the philanthropist phase, wealth and
wisdom are deployed for the service of society and the environment by

means of work of a philanthropic nature. Finally, in the spiritualist phase, the means of advancement once again is education. However, in this final phase, education is gained less through the ordinary senses and more through the mind as a sixth sense, expanding consciousness by gaining intuitive-wisdom from the infinite library of the universe."

I realized that it would be helpful to me to visualize the four phases in a two-by-two matrix. I pulled out a fresh piece of paper and began to sketch. I linked the left axis to the means, which were categorized as education (*vidya*) and work (karma). I linked the right axis to the motives, categorized as gratification of ego (*ahamkara*, false self) and realization of Atma (soul, true Self).

Looking at the Purposeful Life Framework I just created, I realized that there were links between each phase of life and the deepening levels of consciousness described in the Reality-Consciousness-Bliss Framework. I quickly colored in each box with orange, yellow, blue, and violet colors in the related rows of the Reality-Consciousness-Bliss Framework. In the student phase, the student focuses on philosophy, the love ("philos") of knowledge ("sophy"). The student gains information through the senses, and uses this information to create reports. In the professional phase, the focus is on prosperity and wealth. The information gained in the student phase is applied through work to generate results, and is converted to knowledge in the process. In the philanthropist phase, the focus is on philanthropy, the love ("philos") of humanity ("anthropos"). Knowledge gained in the professional phase is applied through philanthropic service for righteousness, and is converted to wisdom in the process. Finally, in the spiritualist phase, the person turns inward and uses intuitive-wisdom to realize the Atma and gain inner peace.

"What happens if someone doesn't go through all four phases?" I asked.

"There is much benefit if the human goes through all four phases," Yogi replied. "However, the society and environment can benefit tremendously even if the human goes through only the first three phases."

"I can understand how both of those scenarios would benefit society, as they go beyond the ego. However, there are four possible scenarios that I can visualize."

I grabbed a new piece of paper and quickly sketched a table to explain these four scenarios.

Purposeful Life Framework (Chart)

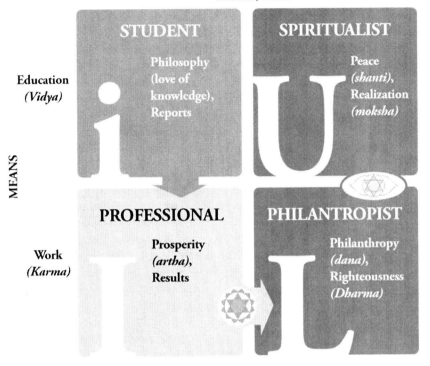

PHASE, Focus

MEANS

Education (Vidya)

Work (Karma)

STUDENT — Philosophy (love of knowledge), Reports

SPIRITUALIST — Peace (shanti), Realization (moksha)

PROFESSIONAL — Prosperity (artha), Results

PHILANTROPIST — Philanthropy (dana), Righteousness (Dharma)

Gratification of Ego (False Self)   **Realization of Atma (Soul, Self)**

MOTIVE

Purposeful Life Framework (Table)

i	'i-shaped' life	Life lived only as a Student, driven by the love (philos-) of knowledge (-sophy). Received investment from society but did not contribute back to society.
I	'I-shaped' life	Progressed from Student phase to Professional phase. Life lived only for the ego ('I') and driven solely by selfish motives. Most people live 'I-shaped' lives.
L	'L-shaped' life	Progressed from Student phase to Professional phase, and then progressed further to the Philanthropist phase, driven by love (philos-) of humanity (-anthropos) and the environment.
U	'U-shaped' life	Progressed through all four phases – from Student to Professional to Philanthropist to Spiritualist, the ideal prescribed by Yoga-Vedanta.

I explained the first scenario to Yogi.

"Someone could be a student for all of her or his life, either by choice or by unfortunate circumstances such as an early death. In such a scenario, the student received an investment from society but never contributed back to society. I am visualizing this as a 'small i-shaped' or 'i-shaped' life.

"The second scenario would be one in which the human lives through the student phase followed by the professional phase. Here, the professional uses the education gained in the previous phase to participate in society. However, the motive is still ego driven. I am visualizing this scenario, going through the first two phases, as a 'large I-shaped' or 'I-shaped' life. I think most people live 'I-shaped' lives."

"Some would state that such a life cannot be considered living," added Yogi, before quoting Swami Vivekananda's powerful words.

"This life is short, the vanities of the world are transient, but they alone live who live for others, the rest are more dead than alive."
—Swami Vivekananda

"One's immediate duty is to provide for one's dependents," continued Yogi. "None is more heartless than a wealthy person who enjoys fine food and clothing without distributing wealth among his or her dependents.[51] As one's wealth increases, one should consider society and all living beings on Earth to be included among one's dependents. That person goes to everlasting hell, which though in possession of wealth, neither gives it away nor enjoys it from greed, saying that he or she has none."[52]

"It follows that reaching the philanthropist and spiritualist phases would be considered true living," I said. "These are the two phases that go beyond the ego or individual consciousness. In the third scenario, the human has progressed through the first three phases, to the philanthropist phase. Here, the person's consciousness has expanded beyond the ego toward Earth Consciousness. I am visualizing this as an 'L-shaped' life. The final scenario, where the person's consciousness has expanded further toward Universal Consciousness, can be referred to as a 'U-shaped' life."

"Why do you call each life trajectory 'i,' 'I,' 'L,' and 'U'?" Yogi asked, looking down at the table I had drawn.

I quickly flipped the page back to the two-by-two matrix I had drawn. "I'm thinking of each phase of life along this chart," I explained. "See? If you stay in the student phase, you only enter one box, so the path is just a brief straight line. Once that extends down into the second box, the professional phase, it becomes a longer straight line. Since both of these phases are ego-driven, I am calling the first path a small i-shaped life and the second path a large I-shaped life. If you move through three phases, the line bends into an 'L' shape. If you move through all four, your path bends to become a 'U' shape."

"What if, after the student phase, the human renounces the world and goes directly to the spiritualist phase?" asked the Yogi.

That scenario had not entered my mind. I took a few moments to think about it before responding. I remembered Swami Vivekananda's words from one of his lectures. He had pointed out that in order for wealth to be deployed for the benefit of society, wealth must first be generated.

> "The householder [or professional] is the basis, the prop, of the whole society; he is the principal earner. ...
> A householder who does not struggle to get wealth is immoral. If he is lazy and content to lead an idle life, he is immoral, because upon him depend hundreds. If he gets riches, hundreds of others will be thereby supported."
> —Swami Vivekananda[53]

"Society invested in such a human's education," I answered Yogi. "However, by renouncing the world immediately after gaining education, this person would have neither participated in nor contributed to society. Such a scenario seems selfish to me since the human did not add any value to society. There may be some exceptions, such as the Buddha, who contributed to society as a teacher after gaining enlightenment. However, this is very rare, and I will not include it in my framework."

At this point, I added some more principles to my list of Yogic Management principles:

Understand that true education teaches humility and builds character, which leads to wealth, Dharma and happiness.

Pursue education and wealth as if you were to live forever. Practice Dharma as if you were to die at any moment.

Live a purposeful life by living an L-shaped or U-shaped life.

I made a corresponding addition to the Yogic Management Mantra.

From living an i-shaped life or I-shaped life, lead me to living an L-shaped life or U-shaped life.

Suddenly, the dog barked. A weighing scale with two pans and a set of cube-shaped weights materialized between Yogi and me. The weights were different colors and were made of different stones and crystals.

"Debts to society must be repaid," replied Yogi. "Society benefits when the values of Dharma, wealth, and pleasure are assigned their proper weights. **Results and wealth are definitely important. But balance is disturbed when results and wealth become more important that righteousness and duty.** I will give you an example. The humans of your time have recently experienced a crisis of global proportions. Tell me what happened."

"Yes," I added. "Starting in 2008, there was a global financial crisis. It affected individuals, organizations, and entire nations that have had to raise funds from external sources to avoid defaulting on their debts. Those who could not had to declare bankruptcy."

"Let's simulate the following scenario," continued Yogi. "Assume that this orange-colored stone symbolizes that which is pleasurable. Assume that this yellow-colored stone symbolizes wealth that you possess."

Yogi placed the yellow and orange stones on the two pans of the weighing scale. The scale tipped down on the side of the yellow stone. "Tell me what happens when the wealth stone is heavier than the pleasure stone."

"If the orange-colored stone symbolizes pleasure, its weight could be thought of as the amount I spend on my expenses and consumption, as well as the amount of debt I have taken on to support my lifestyle. If my wealth (income, savings, assets) exceeds my pleasure (expenses, consumption, debt) I am in good shape. If the orange pleasure stone outweighed the yellow wealth stone, I would be in trouble, just like the people who took a mortgage for a house more expensive than they could afford, or borrowed more on their credit cards than they could pay off."

"Yes," said Yogi. "In simple terms, one must always live within one's means. That pleasure, the pursuit of which does not injure one's Dharma and wealth, should certainly be pursued to one's fill. One should not, however, act like a fool by giving free indulgence to one's senses.[54] One must act to preserve as well as increase one's wealth. If, without seeking to earn, one continues to only spend one's wealth, even if the amount were as large as a mountain in the Himalayas, it would soon be exhausted."[55]

"All of that is sound advice," I said. "But do we need a more complicated approach to the idea of credit and debt? Today's economy is dependent upon consumer spending. If consumers spend less, it will slow down growth in our economy. That could lead to fewer jobs and people could lose the ability to provide for their families."

"Consumption motivated by the gratification of the senses and paid for by debt does not benefit the consumer. The pleasure gained from the gratification of the senses is temporary and, when it passes, the consumer is left with debt. Such debt causes suffering if it cannot be paid. Growth driven by debt and suffering can be detrimental to society, in addition to being wasteful of the Earth's resources."

101

"But what you are recommending is austerity. I don't think many people will be willing to accept a reduction in their quality of life."

"Austerity is simple living that is based on needs and not on wants. It will reduce stress and increase happiness for the individuals and society. And in the process will reduce waste of the Earth's resources. Excessive consumption seldom makes people content or happy."

"You make a valid point," I replied. "The same logic could be scaled up to include organizations and countries. If pleasure outweighs wealth, organizations may become bankrupt and countries may need to default."

Yogi lifted the orange stone from the scale and put it back down on the ground. He picked up a blue stone and held it in front of me. "Assume that this blue stone symbolizes Dharma. Dharma is a more subtle concept than wealth, so when we talk about the 'weight' of Dharma, think in terms of righteousness and not in terms money."

Yogi placed the blue stone on the pan opposite to the yellow stone, and the scale tipped down on the side of the blue stone.

"What happens if Dharma outweighs wealth?" he asked.

"Society benefits when Dharma is treated as more important than wealth," I replied. "Wealth gained through righteous means is beneficial, not just to the person generating the wealth, but also to society and the environment."

I paused for a few moments as I remembered the several instances at Characterra when Raja put profits above ethics and manipulated the system to get approval for unethical plans. The profits had come at the cost of the society and the environment. It was painful to me to remember my role in developing the analysis that the clients had used to make their decisions.

"Society suffers when wealth is treated as more important than Dharma," I added. "Wealth gained through unrighteous means, though it may benefit the individual generating it, causes harm to society and the environment in the process."

"Wealth gained through unrighteous means does not even lead to sustained benefit for those generating it," added Yogi, before quoting multiple sections from the Mahabharata that referred to this topic. "The gap that one seeks to fill with wealth acquired wrongfully remains uncovered, while new ones appear in other places.[56] Prosperity that is acquired through unrighteous acts is soon destroyed, while that which is won by righteous means takes root and descends from generation to generation.[57] Also, prosperity intoxicates even wise and valiant people. Those who live in luxury soon lose their reason."[58]

"So even the individual eventually suffers," I summarized these new teachings.

"Yes. **Profits are important, but not at the cost of principles. Results are important, but not at the cost of righteousness.**"

"But what if wealth gained through unrighteous means is deployed toward philanthropic causes that benefit society and the environment?"

"There are karmic repercussions to unrighteous actions," Yogi answered. "Those perpetrating such acts gain karmic demerit from them. While one person commits unrighteous acts, many reap the advantage resulting therefrom. Yet, in the end, it is the doer alone to whom the demerit of unrighteousness attaches itself, while those who enjoy the fruit escape unhurt.[59] Think of this as a form of karmic history. Unrighteous actions lead to karmic demerit. On the other hand, when you act righteously, you build karmic merit, irrespective of the results. If a person striving to the best of her or his abilities to perform a righteous act meets with failure, I have not the least doubt that the person gains the merit of that act, notwithstanding such failure."[60]

I took some moments to absorb the new teachings. I had heard of credit history and had learned about how to build it. Karmic history, however, was a new and interesting concept.

"Please explain what you mean by 'karmic demerit'," I said. "I thought 'karma' meant 'action' or 'work.'"

"Karma does mean action or work. But it also means the effects caused by actions. Those who gain karmic demerit by performing unrighteous acts will suffer in the future when they become the recipients of unrighteous acts. Sometimes other people also gain the demerit for the unrighteous actions of one individual."

"Please explain."

"In an assembly where an unrighteous act is not rebuked, half the demerit of that act is attached to the head of that assembly, a fourth to the person performing the act, and a fourth to those others who are simply present.[61] Those who witness an unrighteous act and do nothing about it also gain karmic demerit."

I thought about how this would apply in the world of business.

"Let's consider the following scenario," I suggested. "A company has a board of directors, led by the chairman of the board. The board decides to hire an individual to be the CEO of the company. Assume that the board witnesses the CEO propose an unethical undertaking. If they let the CEO proceed with this behavior by doing nothing about it, all board members will gain karmic demerit along with the CEO. Except that the leader of the board, the chairman, will incur twice as much demerit as the CEO and the other board members. Did I understand this correctly?"

"Yes," Yogi confirmed. "This distribution of karmic demerit would apply even to the smallest of teams. The team leader will incur twice the demerit as the team member who performed the unrighteous act and the team members who witnessed it but did nothing about it. The wise have said that if there is a punisher of crimes, people would not dare commit crimes. If there are no punishers, the number of criminals becomes large. If a person who has the power to prevent or punish a crime, does not do so, he or she is also stained by that crime."[62]

I nodded in agreement and added another principle to my list:

Always consider Dharma (righteousness, duty) above wealth (income, savings) and wealth above pleasure (expenses, consumption).

I also added a new line to the Yogic Management Mantra.

From building credit history, lead me to building karmic history.

The weighing scale vanished into golden light.

"Once again, let us discuss balance," continued Yogi. "It is necessary that Dharma, wealth, and pleasure are given the appropriate weight in each person's life. For this to happen, at some point in their lives, professionals need to turn toward philanthropy and work needs to be transformed into service."

"At that point, they need to take a U-turn," I added.

"Correct," added Yogi. "But for philanthropy to be most beneficial to society and the environment, the hierarchy of the body, mind, and spirit need to be taken into consideration. The wise have said that bodily afflictions should be cured with medicines, and the mental ones with spiritual wisdom. This is the power of knowledge.[63] Some forms of philanthropy and service are more beneficial than others. Recall what Swami Vivekenanda had to say on this topic."

The relevant portions of the Swami's speeches entered my mind.

"A spiritually strong and sound man will be strong in every other respect, if he so wishes. Until there is spiritual strength in man even physical needs cannot be well satisfied. Next to spiritual comes intellectual help. The gift of knowledge is a far higher gift than that of food and clothes; it is even higher than giving life to a man, because the real life of man consists of knowledge. Ignorance is death, knowledge is life. Life is of very little value, if it is a life in the dark, groping through ignorance and misery. Next in order comes, of course, helping a man physically. Therefore, in considering the question of helping others, we must always strive not to commit the mistake of thinking that physical help is the only help that can be given. It is not only the last but the least, because it cannot bring about permanent satisfaction. The misery that I feel when I am hungry is satisfied by eating, but hunger returns; my misery can cease only when I am satisfied beyond all want. Then

104

hunger will not make me miserable; no distress, no sorrow will be able to move me. So, that help which tends to make us strong spiritually is the highest, next to it comes intellectual help, and after that physical help."
—Swami Vivekananda[64]

I considered these words to determine how one should prioritize the disbursement of funds so that philanthropy may be of most service, not just to the person receiving the help, but also to society and the environment.

"It would follow that starting or improving a school or university would be a more effective form of philanthropy than starting a food bank," I said, after some thought. "If I had limited funds that I wished to deploy toward charitable causes, I should consider educating a child before feeding a beggar. Would you agree?"

"In all such situations, one must think holistically and use one's power of discernment," replied Yogi. "The beggar fed today would be hungry tomorrow while the child who receives education could become a professional who takes an active role in society. However, if you can educate beggars with the knowledge and skills to gain employment, they would be able to become professionals, participate in society, and feed themselves. In more dire circumstances, if there is widespread poverty in society and people are dying of hunger, the righteous form of philanthropy would be to feed them so that they do not die needlessly."

As I absorbed these concepts, a question still nagged me.

"All your points are valid," I replied. "We have spoken about purpose in terms of the four phases of life. Some say that each person has a purpose or a calling in life. What is mine?"

"One's true purpose is not given to one from the external world," answered Yogi. "One's purpose comes from within. Some people are blessed with a realization about their purpose, which they then choose to pursue. Other people try various paths and listen to many suggestions prior to choosing the purpose they would like to make their own. In either case, one's true purpose is chosen by oneself and not assigned as a task by another. For those who are unsure of their purpose but would like to live a purposeful life, I give a suggestion derived from the verses of the Gita."

Whenever, O descendant of Bharata [Prince Arjuna], there is decline of Dharma, and rise of *adharma* [unrighteousness], then I body Myself forth.
For the protection of the good, for the destruction of the wicked, and for the establishment of Dharma, I come into being in every age.
—Lord Krishna in the Bhagavad Gita, 4.7, 8

105

"These verses refer to the births of *Avatars*," explained Yogi. "An *Avatar* is one who descends from the spiritual world into the material world. Lord Krishna states that when Dharma declines and unrighteousness rises, the One Soul of the Universe takes birth on Earth, incarnated as a human being. The purpose of establishing Dharma is a truly divine purpose. It is for this purpose that *Avatars* like Lord Krishna are born. You too could consider establishing Dharma."

"How can I establish Dharma?" I asked. "I'm not an *Avatar*. I'm just a human being."

Yogi paused to observe two squirrels that just joined our presence. I watched as they picked up some seeds that were next to the dog. Then they climbed a tree that was a few feet away from us.

"Each person can contribute toward establishing Dharma to the best of their abilities," continued Yogi. "No being's contribution is ever wasted. When Lord Rama, the *Avatar* who preceded Lord Krishna, built the Ramasethu Bridge between the mainland of Bharat and the island of Sri Lanka, he was helped by many beings. The apes helped him by placing large rocks, while a squirrel helped by shaking sand from its back onto the bridge. Lord Rama rewarded the squirrel's contribution by stroking its back with his fingers, which formed light-colored stripes. Even in your time, the Indian squirrels bear these stripes. You can contribute what you can for the purpose of establishing Dharma."

"Swami Vivekananda spoke of three ways to help others," I said. "The third way, which was the most important, was giving spiritual help. A spiritually strong person will be strong in the face of any other kind of hardship in her or his life. I spoke of intellectual education. But education can also be spiritual. Spiritual wisdom benefits the individual, society, and environment more than intellectual knowledge. The child who received the intellectual education could turn out to become a successful professional who lives an I-shaped life and does not progress to the philanthropist phase. Worse, the professional could use unethical means to cause harm to society and the environment. If the same child received spiritual education in addition to intellectual education, she or he would progress to the philanthropist phase and make valuable contributions to society and the environment.

"It follows that it is insufficient to teach subjects like finance, marketing, and operations management in the world's business schools. Students at these schools should also learn about ethics, philanthropy, and righteousness. A foundation in Yoga-Vedanta would be invaluable to such students, as well as to society and the environment."

I suddenly felt a feeling of inspiration welling up from somewhere deep within my being. I looked down at my sheaf of papers and then back up at Yogi. "My book," I said quietly.

"Yes?"

"Writing this book, bridging Yoga-Vedanta with Management, could be my contribution toward establishing Dharma," I said, not as a question, but as a realization from within. "I can do this by researching and educating others on these subjects."

The dog barked in approval and Yogi smiled.

"Contribute as best you can toward establishing Dharma," said Yogi. "In this endeavor you will not be alone. Others, with mature minds and awakened Intellects, will help you or make contributions of their own. **Dharma abandons those who abandon Dharma. Dharma protects those who protect Dharma.**"[65]

Yogi paused for a few moments before continuing.

"Here's a question for you," he said. "If you were to give a solution in one word to the majority of problems afflicting humans and all living beings on Earth, what would it be? Your solution should impact all living beings, for charity consists in protecting all creatures."[66]

I thought for several moments and took into consideration what I had learned from the Gita and Yogi before giving the answer.

"Dharma," I replied. "**Dharma is the one word solution to most of the problems afflicting the human species and all life on Earth. In our ignorance, we have treated wealth as more important than Dharma, prosperity as more important than philanthropy, and results as more important than righteousness. We equate success with monetary gains and have given people the incentive to be greedy instead of balanced in their actions. Our greed has led to prosperity for a few individuals at the cost of poverty for everyone else, the destruction of the environment, and the suffering of all living species that make up the macro-organism we call the Earth.**

"The world of business believes that it is accountable solely to its shareholders and owners. In reality, all living beings on Earth are impacted by the practices of the business world, and hence are the real stakeholders that leaders and managers should consider in all decision making. If Dharma can be practiced in the world of business and taught at business schools, it will greatly benefit humans and all living beings on Earth."

Yogi nodded. "You have understood the importance of Dharma. One further point you must understand is that you cannot force a person to practice Dharma. You cannot force a person to behave in a righteous, ethical, peaceful, or compassionate manner. Such behavior comes from within and is a manifestation of that human's consciousness. Dharma is established when human consciousness rises to transcend fear, greed, insatiable desire, anger, jealousy, and all such behaviors that stem from ignorance. When one understands the oneness and interconnectivity of all beings, applies wisdom in addition to knowledge, considers righteousness and ethics in addition to results and the law, principles and peace in addition to profits and pleasure, then one automatically becomes a practitioner of Dharma."

I summarized these teachings into a principle.

Establish Dharma in the world of business by practicing Yogic Management.

Suddenly, a flock of swans descended from the sky and landed a few feet away from us. They spent some moments interacting with the dog, who seemed to be their friend, and then went to the lake. It was a beautiful sight.

"Yogi," I said, as the swans walked away. "You mentioned that at some point in their lives, professionals need to turn toward philanthropy and work needs to be transformed into service. Please tell me about this turning point in human consciousness."

12. *Anahata*: The Turning Point

"It is at the turning point that one becomes a human being," said Yogi. "To understand this concept, let's review verses from the Upanishad, which refer to the One supreme being as *Prajapati* (Lord of Creatures)."

> *Prajapati* had three kinds of offspring: gods [*devas*], men [humans] and demons (*asuras*). They lived with *Prajapati*, practising the vows of *brahmacharins* [the student phase].
> After finishing their term, the gods said to him:
> "Please instruct us, Sir." To them he uttered the syllable da and asked: "Have you understood?"
> They replied: "We have. You said to us, 'Control yourselves (*damyata*).'"
> He said: "Yes, you have understood."
> Then the men said to him: "Please instruct us, Sir" To them he uttered the same syllable da and asked: "Have you understood?"
> They replied: "We have. You said to us, 'Give (*datta*).'" He said: "Yes, you have understood."
> Then the demons said to him: "Please instruct us, Sir." To them he uttered the same syllable da and asked: "Have you understood?"
> They replied: "We have. You said to us: 'Be compassionate (*dayadhvam*).'" He said: "Yes, you have understood."
> That very thing is repeated even today by the heavenly voice, in the form of thunder, as "Da," "Da," "Da," which means: "Control yourselves," "Give," and "Have compassion."
> Therefore one should learn these three: self-control, giving and mercy.
> —Brihadaranyaka Upanishad 5.2.1 – 3

"Yogi, the order of these three instructions seems significant," I said. "Self-control is higher than charity, which is higher than compassion. They seem to echo the hierarchy in consciousness that we discussed in relation to the Purposeful Life Framework.

"The One advises the humans to be charitable to others. The demons are beings that don't behave like humans do. They are advised to develop compassion toward other beings. These two types of beings are living i-shaped or I-shaped lives, focused on ego gratification. But the turning point in consciousness is the point when the individual becomes compassionate to other beings, and being charitable helps the individual progress from the professional phase to the philanthropist phase. Behaving charitably means living an L-shaped life. In order to be genuinely charitable, one must first be compassionate to other beings. Compassion would thus be a prerequisite to charity."

"You are thinking in the right direction," replied Yogi. "I will now give you another tool for visualizing the rising levels of consciousness. In Yoga, there are seven primary chakras or wheels. These are seven energy centers that are located along the spine, starting at the base of the spine and progressing to the crown of the head."

I listened closely to Yogi's explanation of the seven chakras and created an image and a chart.

Seven Chakras (Image)

Seven Chakra Chart

Crown *(Sahasrara)* Chakra

Symbolized as a violet-colored lotus with a thousand petals.
Linked with bliss and the realization of Atma.

Third Eye *(Ajna)* Chakra

Symbolized as an indigo-colored lotus with two petals.
Linked with intuition and psychic abilities.

Throat *(Vishuddha)* Chakra

Symbolized as a blue- or turquoise-colored lotus with sixteen petals.
Linked with communication and discernment.

Heart *(Anahata)* Chakra

Symbolized as a green-colored lotus with twelve petals.
Linked with compassion and love.

Solar Plexus *(Manipura)* Chakra

Symbolized as a yellow-colored lotus with ten petals.
Linked with strength, power and the ego.

Sacral *(Svadhishthana)* Chakra

Symbolized as an orange-colored lotus with six petals.
Linked with feelings and sensations.

Root *(Muladhara)* Chakra

Symbolized as a red-colored lotus with four petals.
Linked with instinct and survival.

"Each chakra has its own frequency," Yogi explained. "The frequency of vibrations for each chakra increases from the root chakra to the crown chakra. The root chakra is the densest in terms of vibration and is depicted in red, the color with the lowest frequency in the visible spectrum. The sacral chakra is more subtle in vibration and is depicted in orange. The chakras progress from dense to subtle. The crown chakra is depicted in violet, the color with the highest frequency in the visible spectrum.

"A powerful energy lies dormant in the red-colored root chakra," Yogi explained. "In this chakra, this energy is coiled in circles."

"Like the *Chakravyuh*, the wheel-shaped battle formation used in the Mahabharata!" I exclaimed "I have this recurring dream. I am running in circles around a road of reddish-brown earth. I am running with my brother, Karan, my boss, Raja, and many other colleagues, relatives, and former classmates. We are all wearing red."

"Yes, your dream is connected to the *Chakravyuh*. In that battle formation, the warriors were dressed in red. In your dream, you are trapped in an unexamined life. You can only react and keep running; you are not able to take a broader perspective on life or your purpose for living.

"Once you can raise your consciousness, your energy will ascend to the higher chakras. When one becomes compassionate to other beings, the heart chakra becomes unblocked."

"So, the *turning point* in human consciousness is the unblocking of the heart (*anahata*) chakra!" It was all coming together. I pulled out the page with the Purposeful Life Framework again. "This turning point is the point where one moves from the professional phase to the philanthropist phase. I'll draw the green symbol of the heart chakra between these two phases."

As I stared down at the matrix, something else occurred to me. "Yogi, I'm starting to realize that each of the four phases is linked to four of the seven chakras. In the Student Phase, education is gained through the five ordinary senses of perception. I am going to color this square in orange, like the sacral chakra, which is linked to sensations. I will color the professional phase in yellow, like the solar plexus chakra, which is linked to strength, power, and the ego. I will color the philanthropist phase in blue, like the throat chakra, which is linked to discernment. I have placed the symbol for the green heart chakra on the boundary line between the professional and philanthropist phases. That brings us to the sixth chakra, the third eye chakra. I'm not entirely sure where to put it. Should I color the spiritualist phase the same color as the third eye chakra or the crown chakra?"

"The third eye chakra is linked to intuition and psychic abilities," said Yogi. "When it is unblocked, the being is able to access the infinite library of the universe through intuition. The crown chakra is the seventh and last chakra. It is linked to bliss and the realization of the Atma."

"I think I understand," I said. "The third eye chakra is a bottleneck, just like the heart chakra. I can depict this indigo-colored chakra between the philanthropist phase and the spiritualist phase. When this chakra is unblocked, the human can progress to the spiritualist phase, which I will color in violet, like the crown chakra. It follows that, the *transcending point* in human consciousness is the unblocking of the third eye (*ajna*) chakra!"

The Purposeful Life Framework was now complete in my mind. I then went back to my Reality-Consciousness-Bliss Framework. I began to link the body, senses, mind, Intellect, and bliss sheath to the colors red, orange, yellow, blue, and violet, respectively. I also drew in the heart chakra at the 3.0 milestone. Only when it is unblocked will one's consciousness rise beyond individual consciousness, to team consciousness and beyond, all the way to Earth Consciousness. Correspondingly, when it is unblocked, one can go from knowledge to wisdom, from results to righteousness, and from prosperity to philanthropy. I added the third eye chakra at the 4.0 milestone. When it is unblocked, consciousness will rise beyond the material world of Earth Consciousness toward the spiritual world of Universal Consciousness. Correspondingly, when it is unblocked, one can go from wisdom to intuitive-wisdom, from righteousness to the realization of the Atma, and from philanthropy to inner peace. Thus the Reality-Consciousness-Bliss Framework was also complete.

"When the heart chakra is being unblocked, it can be a painful experience," explained Yogi after giving me some moments to complete the frameworks. "Many have experienced a personal or moral crisis during the process."

"Why?"

"Because the ego resists this transformation of the being. The ego thrives when the flow of consciousness is restricted to the lower three chakras. It can be in power only when the mind is immature and childish. But when the heart chakra is unblocked, energy flows through the heart and throat Chakras. The Intellect is awakened and in control of the mind, ego, and other five senses when energy rises to the throat chakra, which is linked to the power of discernment. The ego is put in its place by the Intellect that has been awakened. The ego can influence the mind, which faces the external world and senses. But it cannot control an awakened Intellect, which faces the spiritual world and Atma. For this reason, the ego puts up a fight. The crisis that occurs is the conflict between the ego (*ahamkara*, false self) and the Atma (soul, true Self). I think you went through the same crisis."

"Yes," I replied, after relating the concept to my crisis. "I had the crisis when I had to choose between results and righteousness at Characterra."

"Your Intellect is now awakened," continued Yogi. "Always be aware of your ego. It tries to block your advancement. One of the ways it does so, without you realizing it, is when you deal with criticism. Criticism, if discerned by the Intellect, can lead to growth and improvement. But the ego, which is fickle in nature, does not like to take criticism. When you speak or write about Yogic Management, you will receive both praise and criticism. How will you deal with criticism?"

"I will listen to my critics. If they are making valid points, I will make changes and improve myself. However, I may find it difficult to accept criticism that is harsh in tone. How should I deal with these kinds of criticisms?"

"The ego concerns itself with the tone of the message. The Intellect cares about the content of the message and not the tone in which it is delivered. If the criticism is valid and beneficial, irrespective of whether the tone is harsh and unpleasant, you should accept it. Treat such criticism as you would treat foul tasting medicine, which you need to take in order to heal from an illness. If criticism is understood with discernment, it can bring great benefits through self-improvement."

"What if the criticism is false in content and malicious in intent? What if my points are valid, but I draw criticism because my critic has an agenda to prove or is just plain evil in nature?"

"Consider the behavior of the swan and the behavior of the pig," Yogi replied. "You have observed the behavior of the swan and saw how it can discern between milk-like sap and water. Now observe our new friend."

Yogi pointed in the direction of a flower patch that was a few feet away from us. It was filled with colorful flowers that were giving out pleasant scents. A pig walked past us to the flower bed. It looked like it just had a lot of fun rolling around in some dirt. It sniffed and dug around the roots of the plants while ignoring the flowers.

"Some of your critics will behave like this swine," said Yogi. "Just as the swine always look for dirt and filth even in the midst of a flower garden, so will the wicked always choose the toxic out of both the toxic and the pure that others speak. The wise, on hearing the speeches of others that are intermixed with both purity and toxicity, accept only what is pure, like swans that always extract only milk, though it be mixed with water."[67]

The pig sniffed around and dug a little longer. Not finding what it was searching for, it left our presence and took its search elsewhere.

"Humans are imperfect beings," continued Yogi. "No human is completely pure or completely toxic. When you listen or read the words of others, behave like the swan and use your Intellect to discern their words. Learn and grow by absorbing what is pure and beneficial to you. Ignore the toxic words, just as the lotus lets water slide away from its leaf. Your words too will be mixed with purity and toxicity. Your critics, whose consciousnesses are at the level of swine, will only focus on your faults. Your wise critics will make note of what you say that is beneficial to them, society, and the environment. Focus your efforts on the wise and righteous, upon whom depends the future."

Yogi paused for a few moments to let me absorb these concepts.

"The ego is also the root of jealousy," continued Yogi, on the topic of the ego. "It is immature and gets upset when it perceives the success or happiness of other people. In order to make itself feel better it reacts by pulling others down. By thinking and speaking ill of successful or happy people and by bringing them down to its own level of non-achievement and unhappiness, the ego deludes itself into feeling superior. Toxic thoughts and speech aimed at others have a tendency to rebound in the form of negative energy redirected to the source of toxicity. It is easier to criticize the achievements of another than to resolve and act to achieve one's true potential. The Intellect, unlike the ego, understands this thought. Those who possess a mature Intellect will use their inner strength to raise themselves instead of wasting their energy on pulling others down."

"You make valid points," I replied.

"Words spoken or written, like deeds performed, have karmic repercussions for those who create them," Yogi explained further. "Karmic demerit is attached to speaking words that are malicious in content or harsh in tone, as well as to words that the speaker knows to be false. The same is true for written words. Ignorant people seek to injure the wise by false reproaches and evil speeches. The consequence is that they take upon themselves the demerit of the wise, while the latter, freed from their demerits, are forgiven.[68] A wise person who has been injured by another's wordy arrows, should, even if deeply wounded and burning with pain, bear the words patiently. The wise person should do so remembering that she or he gains the slanderer's merits."[69]

"I understand that words contribute to a person's karmic history, just as actions do," I reiterated. "Thanks for pointing that out."

"We have spoken of criticism," Yogi continued. "Let's talk of praise. What if, after all your hard work and contributions, you do not receive any praise or respect?"

"It feels good to be praised. I would be disappointed to not receive any, especially if I have put in a lot of effort and made impactful contributions. How would you advise someone who faces such a scenario?"

"Think of praise in terms of the pleasant and criticism in terms of the beneficial," advised Yogi. "Praise is pleasant and boosts the ego. But it does not help you improve. Criticism is unpleasant and upsets the ego. Yet it can be a source of self-improvement. The ego thrives on praise. Just as it does not like to take criticism, the ego gets upset when there is a lack of praise. In such situations, the Intellect should use the power of discernment to ensure that the ego does not interfere. The wise should never exult at receiving honors nor should they grieve at insults.[70] One should never regard oneself as honored who is honored by others. One should not, therefore, grieve when one is not honored by others. People act according to their nature just as they open and shut their eyelids. It is only the learned who pay respect to others. They who are ignorant, unrighteous, or deceitful, never pay respect to those who are worthy of respect. On the other hand, they always show disrespect to such persons.[71] Now, how would you apply your—" Yogi shuffled through the pages I was holding until he got to the one he was looking for "—Knowledge Work Equation to a scenario in which you have not received the praise you deserve?"

"Knowledge + Action = Results," I replied. "Looking for praise means focusing on the RHS of the equation. Instead I should focus on the LHS, on doing the work while remaining non-attached to the results (fruits) of the work. I must focus on my contribution through work rather than on the material results obtained from work."

I paused for a few moments to absorb these new ideas.

"We have discussed the seven chakras," Yogi said. "We have identified the heart chakra to be a bottleneck in the rise of consciousness and have determined that the unblocking of this chakra is the turning point between the professional phase and the philanthropist phase. Now it is time for me to explain the system that will help you raise your consciousness from the lower three chakras to the higher chakras. Yogis refer to this system as the Royal Road or the Yoga on Meditation (Raja-Yoga)."

13. The Royal Road

"As discussed, the concepts and techniques of Yoga are very ancient," said Yogi. "Over two thousand years before your time, a great sage took upon himself an important task. This sage, Maharishi Patanjali, wrote the Yoga Sutras, in order to preserve, compile, and arrange the important teachings in a format that would help students and practitioners. Even in your time, the Yoga Sutras and the Bhagavad Gita are considered to be the two texts that contain the essential teachings of the four classical Yogas."

Yogi and I had been discussing the Yoga of Knowledge and the Yoga of Action. I was now going to learn the third Yoga, the Yoga of Meditation, often referred to as the Royal Road.

"Maharishi Patanjali's Yoga Sutras is a concise compilation consisting of 196 aphorisms," added Yogi. "When you read this compilation, you will notice the similarity in teachings with the Upanishads, Gita, and Mahabharata texts. These texts predate the Yoga Sutras and explain many yogic concepts in greater detail. Notice the similarity between what we have already discussed and the famous definition of Yoga given in the second aphorism."

Yoga is restraining the vibrations of the mind
—Yoga Sutras, Chapter 1, Aphorism 2

This definition was similar to the Gita (2.48) definition: "Yoga is evenness or balance of mind." It was also similar to the Katha Upanishad (2.3.11) definition: "the firm control of the senses is what is called Yoga."

"In other aphorisms, the Maharishi explains the Yoga of Meditation in terms of eight branches (*ashtanga*)," continued Yogi. "The following aphorism lists the eight branches. And the two that follow explain the first two branches."

Maharishi Patanjali's Eight Branches of Yoga

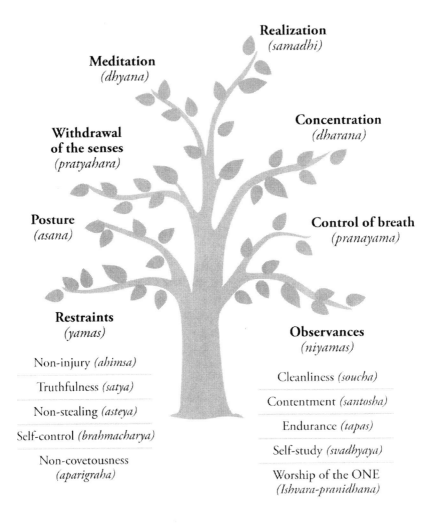

Restraints (*yamas*), observances (*niyamas*), posture (*asana*), control of breath (*pranayama*), withdrawal of the senses (*pratyahara*), concentration (*dharana*), meditation (*dhyana*) and realization (*samadhi*).
—Yoga Sutras, Chapter 2, Aphorism 29

Non-injury (*ahimsa*), truthfulness (*satya*), non-stealing (*asteya*), continence (*brahmacharya*) and non-covetousness (*aparigraha*) are the restraints (*yamas*).
—Yoga Sutras, Chapter 2, Aphorism 30

Internal and external cleanliness (*soucha*), contentment (*santosha*), endurance (*tapas*), self-study (*svadhyaya*) and the worship of God (*ishvara-pranidhana*) are the observances (*niyamas*).
—Yoga Sutras, Chapter 2, Aphorism 32

Once more, to help me remember and better understand the eight branches, I created an image.

"The eight branches are an excellent roadmap for students and practitioners of Yoga," Yogi explained. "Their practice leads to the rise in consciousness as energy flows from the lower chakras to the higher chakras. Those who have renounced the world, as well as those in the spiritualist phase of life, should be strict about the practices. The yogis who have chosen to participate in the world, in the student, professional, and philanthropist phases, can use their discernment to decide to what extent they can adhere to these practices. A practical balance must be reached so that the yogi can advance her or his consciousness, while still contributing to society, the environment, and her or his dependents. Let's start our discussion with the five abstentions."

1. ABSTENTIONS

Non-injury

"The first restraint is non-injury (*ahimsa*)," said Yogi. "The wise have said that non-injury is the highest Dharma.[72] The eternal duty of the righteous toward all creatures is never to injure them in thought, word, and deed, but to bear them love and give them their due."[73]

"Non-injury to all creatures?" I asked.

"Yes. All livings beings are One with Brahman, the eternal, infinite and never changing Soul of the Universe."

"It is impossible to not injure any creature. Even ordinary activities like walking, talking, and eating fruits and vegetables will lead to the death of micro-organisms."

"That is true. But you can try your best to avoid injuring others."

A doubt then entered my mind.

"Let's assume that I write a book on Yogic Management," I said. "Many people will get to learn about the concepts, principles, and frameworks we have discussed. When they do, they may become more vigilant of whether their actions are injuring others and may make greater efforts to avoid causing injury. However, in the process of printing these books, trees will need to be cut down for paper and toxic chemicals will need to be used to process the paper and produce the ink. This causes harm to the environment and will cause injury to humans and other beings that are impacted. Would this act of harming the environment and injuring some beings in order to make others aware of Yogic Management be considered an act of injury or non-injury?"

"The wise have said the following," answered Yogi. "When unrighteousness assumes the aspect of righteousness and righteousness assumes the aspect of unrighteousness, and righteousness again appears in its true form, they who are learned should discern between the two by means of their Intellects."[74]

I resolved to use my Intellect and power of discernment when faced with difficult questions, like the one I brought up. With regard to publishing books, a solution can be found through technology. An electronic book (ebook) that can be read on tablets, phones, computers, and other electronic devices would be a more sustainable and environmentally friendly alternative to books printed on paper.

As for the problems I was facing at Characterra, I discerned that to prevent injury to the organization, society, and the environment, it was going to be necessary to injure Raja's ego.

Truthfulness

"The second restraint is truthfulness (*satya*)," said Yogi. "Truthfulness is to be practiced in thought, word, and deed. Although this appears to be a straightforward abstention, it too requires an awakened Intellect and the application of discernment. Because something is the literal truth, that does not mean that you should say it, just so that you can injure others. Your motive for speaking the truth should be pure. Silence is superior to speaking the literal truth, if the motive for speaking the truth is to injure other beings."

"Is that why non-injury is the first abstention and truthfulness is the second?" I asked.

"Yes. One's motive should be to help other beings. The speaking of truth is good, and the knowledge of truth may also be good. But what is conducive to achieving the greatest good for all creatures is known as the highest truth."[75]

Non-stealing

"The third restraint is non-stealing," continued Yogi. "Non-stealing does not apply just to wealth and objects. It also applies to more subtle things like education, information, and work."

"Plagiarism and piracy would be considered theft," I added. "As would taking credit for the work done by a colleague."

"Yes. As is the case with other acts of unrighteousness, karmic demerit attaches itself to one who steals. What would you do if a deceitful colleague manipulated a situation and took credit for work that you did?"

"The righteous thing for me to do would be to give my colleague the chance to correct the falsehood," I replied after some thought. "If my colleague does not heed my suggestion, I must inform the managers and leaders about the reality of the situation. If I don't, the deceitful colleague could be given greater responsibility that he or she is not qualified to handle. It is in the best interest of the organization if the most qualified persons are in roles with greater responsibilities. An employee who lacks a good character should not be given such roles. If necessary, such employees should be let go, as their very presence could be toxic to the organization."

"You have grown in your thinking. Always remember that each situation can be handled by an awakened Intellect and the power of discernment."

Self-control

"The fourth restraint is self-control toward the gratification of the senses," added Yogi. "For those who have renounced the world and for those in the spiritualist phase of life, self-control means abstention from all sensual pleasures. For those who have chosen to participate in the world, it translates to moderation in activities that gratify the senses. When one controls one's senses, one can channel one's energy toward intellectual and spiritual advancement."

Non-covetousness

"The last restraint is non-covetousness," said Yogi. "One must not covet that which belongs to others or be greedy and hoard more than what one needs. The wise, knowing the instability of youth, beauty, life, wealth, prosperity, and the company of loved ones, never covet them."[76]

2. OBSERVANCES

Internal and external cleanliness

"Let's now discuss the five observances, the second of the eight branches," Yogi said. "The first observance is cleanliness, which includes both internal and external cleanliness. It is not sufficient to take a thorough bath to clean the body. The wise have said that a true bath consists in washing the mind clean of all impurities."[77]

"This can be achieved by the constant practice of righteous and pure thoughts," I added. "And by keeping the mind unattached to the toxicity around us, as the lotus leaf lets water flow off it freely."

"Yes. You will notice that many of the concepts you have learned before are connected to the restraints and observances. Yoga also has some effective detoxification techniques. One in particular that can help you with your health is nasal irrigation (*jala neti*). In addition to detoxification, this technique leads to mental alertness, which will improve the productivity of work done with the mind and Intellect."

Yogi demonstrated the technique by using clean salt water and a *neti* pot. He tilted his head at an angle and then poured water from the *neti* pot through one nostril and out through the other while breathing through his mouth. He then repeated the process for the other nostril.

Contentment

"The second observance is contentment," Yogi explained further. "Only the ignorant are discontented. The wise are always content. The thirst of wealth can never be satisfied. Contentment is the highest happiness. Therefore, the wise regard contentment as the highest object of pursuit."[78]

"Some believe that discontentment is the root of prosperity," I said, remembering Raja's mentorship. "They say that discontentment motivates one to achieve greater things."

"Being content does not mean that one becomes complacent and lazy. One must work hard and perform one's duties. Think once more about your Knowledge Work Equation."

"One must focus on the knowledge and actions and on what one can contribute through work," I replied. "One must be content with the results obtained from work, thus being non-attached to the fruits of work."

"Yes. One must not give way to discontent, for it is like a virulent poison."[79]

Endurance

"The third observance is endurance," Yogi added. "One must willingly and calmly endure the pairs of opposites of life—happiness and misery, success and failure, purity and toxicity, pleasant and unpleasant, and so forth. Endurance also involves austere practices, such as reducing one's needs and desires, controlling one's ego, and engaging in philanthropic activities for the sake of others."

"Austerity builds endurance?" I asked.

"Yes, it does. Physical, intellectual, and spiritual strength is gained through the development of endurance."

Self-study

"The fourth observance is self-study," Yogi continued. "One must regularly study the sacred texts and scriptures. As discussed earlier, one can build one's character and change one's way of thinking by filling the mind with thoughts that are illuminating, pure, and righteous. Great advancement can be gained by studying texts like the Upanishads and Bhagavad Gita."

Worship of the ONE

"The fifth and last observance is the worship of the One Soul of the Universe," Yogi continued. "Maharishi Patanjali refers to the One as Ishvara, the deity that personifies the formless, eternal, infinite, and indivisible Brahman. Brahman has no attributes. But Ishvara has a human form and attributes that the limited human mind can visualize and focus on. This final observance involves faithful surrender to the One. This surrender is a form of humility and acknowledgement that you are a small part of an infinitely large macro-organism."

3. POSTURE

"This brings us to posture (*asana*), the third of the eight branches," Yogi proceeded. "One's posture must be firm and pleasant. What comes to mind when most people think of Yoga?"

"Most people think of Yoga as exercises that involve a lot of stretching and bending," I replied.

"What they are referring to is the third branch, posture," continued Yogi. "One must sit straight, with the head, neck, and spine aligned with each other. The right postures can help the Yogi make progress in concentration, meditation, and realization. Not much is mentioned about posture in the Yoga Sutras. But other later texts have explained a variety of postures. Millions of Yoga practitioners across the world now practice these postures and have benefited tremendously through improved health. As discussed in the chariot analogy, the physical body is the vehicle for the Atma. A healthy body helps one become more productive, not just in work involving the body, but also in work involving the mind and Intellect. Would you like to meet a great Yogi who revived these postures and was a major part of their spread throughout the world?"

"Absolutely," I answered.

The dog barked. Once again, the three of us were covered with golden light and then transported through time and space. As the golden light disappeared, I began to notice that we were by mountains and a magnificent river. This was definitely India, but I was not sure where in India.

"Where are we?" I asked.

"Rishikesh, by the river Ganga, in the foothills of the Himalayas," replied Yogi.

"When?"

"1955."

We made our way to an ashram that housed a spiritual organization called The Divine Life Society. Once there, we met the founder, Swami Sivananda, who gave us a warm welcome. The Swami was a great yogi and guru, who had played an important role in the revival of Yoga in the twentieth century. Yogi asked the Swami to teach me postures, as well as the control of breath, the fourth branch of Yoga. The Swami gladly trained me, along with his students. During my training I got to interact with several of the disciples, all of whom were intelligent and talented. I had some excellent conversations with four students in particular: Swami Vishnudevananda, Swami Satyananda, Swami Chinmayananda, and Swami Satchidananda. All went on to make incredible contributions toward the rise in human consciousness by setting up some of the greatest Yoga-Vedanta schools in the world.

"An ounce of practice is worth tons of theory," said Swami Sivananda, when I started my training.

There are several hundred postures that a Yogi can learn and practice. The Swami selected a subset of these postures that were an effective and balanced combination. The warm up routine was the Sun Salutation (*Surya Namaskara*), a series of twelve positions that brought amazing flexibility to the spine and limbs. This was followed by carefully selected postures that I found to be very beneficial in helping me to focus my mind. These postures included the headstand, shoulderstand, plough, fish, cobra, bow and spinal twist.[80]

4. BREATH CONTROL

After going through the postures, Swami Sivananda began to teach me breath control (*pranayama*) techniques, the fourth of the eight branches.

"Breath control techniques are very ancient," Yogi mentioned. "It was even practiced at the time of the Mahabharata.[81] Recall the second of the five sheaths of the body."

I quickly flipped through my papers until I found the concentric circles I'd drawn. "It was the life-force (*prana*) or breath sheath," I said. "This exists between the physical sheath and the mind sheath."

"It is between these sheaths because breath is the bridge between the body and mind. When you control your breath, you can connect the body to the mind and bring balance to both. If faced with any stressful situation in which your mind and body are agitated, start to control your breath and you will be able to calm your mind and body."

Swami Sivananda smiles and nods. He takes me through two forms of breath control exercises:

1.   Cleansing breathing (*Kapalabhati*)
2.   Alternate nostril breathing (*Anuloma Viloma*)

I found both exercises to be very effective in linking the body and the mind. As I finished my training with Swami Sivananda, he gave me some final words of advice on Yoga.

"Simple living and high thinking," said the Swami.

I thanked him for his teachings. Then the dog, Yogi, and I were transported back to the ancient settlement by the Himalayas.

5. WITHDRAWAL OF THE SENSES

"You have learned about restraints, observances, postures, and the control of breath," Yogi said. "These prepare the Yogi for the more subtle practices that follow. We will now discuss the fifth branch, the withdrawal of the senses. A posture very suitable for this is the lotus posture (*padmasana*). This posture will also help you with concentration, meditation, and realization."

Yogi demonstrated the lotus posture and then I tried it. The posture involved sitting cross-legged on the floor, with the head, neck, and spine aligned with each other. After I had learned this posture, Yogi diverted my attention to a new visitor.

"Now, observe our friend from the animal kingdom," Yogi said.

He pointed at a tortoise that was walking a few feet away from us. Suddenly the weather became windy and dust and leaves started flowing through the air. I closed my eyelids partially, but kept them open enough to observe the tortoise as it withdrew its limbs into its shell. When the wind became calm a few moments later, the tortoise exited the shell and went its way. A verse from the Gita then entered my mind.

When also, like the tortoise its limbs, he [the Yogi] can completely withdraw the senses from their objects, then his wisdom becomes steady.
—Lord Krishna in the Bhagavad Gita, 2.58

"Before meditation and realization, one must learn to withdraw one's senses," explained Yogi. "As discussed earlier, this can be a challenge as the senses constantly send inputs from the material/external world to the mind. But this challenge can be overcome by practice and awareness. If you shut your eyes and focus on your sense of hearing, you will notice that you can hear more than you would with your eyes open. What would happen if all of the five ordinary senses were withdrawn?"

"The power of the sixth sense, the mind, would be heightened," I replied. "Its focus would not be external, on the material world. It would focus internally, in the direction of the spiritual world."

6.–8. CONCENTRATION, MEDITATION, AND REALIZATION

"The withdrawal of the senses leads to the sixth branch, concentration," Yogi continued. "It involves focusing the mind on an internal or external object. Meditation is the state of mind achieved when the mind succeeds in focusing on the object uninterrupted for some time. This leads to realization or absorption, when the mind merges with the object. In your time, one tradition of meditation has been revived and popularized around the world. This is the Buddha's *vipassana* meditation."

After listening to the instructions, I practiced meditation. I gained peace of mind and body. And I also gained some intuitive-wisdom by using my mind as a sixth sense to access the infinite library of the universe. But I did not realize the Atma. That would take a lot more practice.

"Theory is not enough," added Yogi. "It is necessary, but is no substitution for practice, experimentation, and meditation. The wise have said that argument leads to no certain conclusion. The scriptures are different from one another and there is not even one sage whose opinion can be accepted by all. The truth about righteousness and duty is hidden in caves. Therefore, seclusion and withdrawal is the path along which the great have traveled.[82] For thousands of years, Yogis have chosen to meditate in secluded spots, like caves. Through their efforts, many have achieved the realization of the Atma."

14. Work, War, and Worship

"The Yoga of Meditation is indeed a magnificent system to follow," I said, after writing out a quick summary of Maharishi Patanjali's eight branches. "I can already feel the benefits of practicing this Yoga and am convinced that it will help me raise my consciousness from the lower chakras to the higher ones. But you also mentioned *vipassana* meditation that was created by the Buddha. Is it true that he did not preach Vedic philosophies?"

"The Buddha did not accept the authority of the Vedas," replied Yogi. "But his teachings were rooted in Dharma. There are several schools in the Dharma traditions. The Sanskrit texts do not contain the word 'Hindu' because this is a word derived later from the Indus River. What the texts refer to is simply Dharma, or more specifically *Sanatana* (Eternal) Dharma, which is the authentic name of the tradition referred to as Hinduism in your time. *Sanatana* Dharma is categorized into six orthodox schools, the major ones being Yoga and Vedanta. These orthodox schools accept the authority of the Vedas, the most ancient of Sanskrit texts. There are also heterodox schools, such as Buddhism and Jainism, which share philosophies with the orthodox schools, but do not accept the authority of the Vedas. The Buddha taught about Dharma, karma, meditation, and a variety of concepts that predated him by several millennia. A yogi can benefit by practicing *vipassana* and the other teachings of the Buddha."

"A question just entered my mind on the last observance, which is the worship of the One Soul of the Universe," I said. "I understand that the formless, eternal, infinite, and indivisible Brahman is Ishvara, when personified in a form that the limited human mind can visualize and focus on. In essence, the philosophies of Yoga-Vedanta deal with One Supreme Being. Why, then, does modern Hinduism have multiple deities that people worship?"

"Deities are symbolic representations of various aspects of Brahman," answered Yogi. "Review these verses."

Without and within (all) beings; the unmoving and also the moving; because of Its subtlety incomprehensible; It is far and near.
Impartible [indivisible], yet It exists as if divided in beings: It is to be known as sustaining beings; and devouring, as well as generating (them).
—Lord Krishna in the Bhagavad Gita, 13.15, 16

127

"Here we learn that the One sustains, devours, and generates all beings," continued Yogi. "The Soul of the Universe has three forms. In the form of Brahma, he is the Creator; in the form of Vishnu, he is the Preserver; and in his form as Shiva, he is the Destroyer of the Universe.[83] These three deities make up the *trimurti* (three forms) of Brahman and are the main deities in modern Hinduism."

I recalled something I had learned as a child on the roles performed by three main deities. Brahma, not to be confused with Brahman, is the deity of generation who creates all beings. Vishnu is the deity that operates the universe or sustains all life. Shiva is the deity of destruction, through whom the old makes way for the new.

"Generator + Operator + Destroyer = GOD," I added. "Each is an aspect of Brahman represented in a different form."

"Yes," Yogi replied. "The One is indivisible. Yet It exists in all beings. Everything in the universe is a manifestation of the One. This brings us to the fourth of the four Yogas. You have learned about the Yogas of Knowledge, Action, and Meditation. The fourth is the Yoga of Devotion (Bhakti-Yoga). This is the simplest form of Yoga. It can be done with prayer and with the aid of mantras as well as symbols (*yantras*). These help the practitioner focus the mind on their chosen deity, an image of the One. Through devotion, faith, and love for the One, the heart chakra can be unblocked."

"Isn't it inaccurate to worship an image, though?" I asked.

"Many people find it helpful to focus their minds on an image or being. It is easier to focus on a personal ideal for the One than it is to focus on the formless Soul of the Universe."

Yogi then taught me some mantras and symbols that helped focus the mind. The Gayatri Mantra, in particular, was one that I found to be very powerful and beneficial.

"Some caution is necessary with the Yoga of Devotion," advised Yogi. "The love for one ideal can sometimes lead to the hate of other ideals. Hate leads to conflict and war. Therefore, when you practice worship, ensure that the ideal you are focusing on expands the reach of your love and compassion rather than narrowing it."

"Sound advice," I replied, as I recalled a line that I had previously added to the Yogic Management Mantra: 'from performing work as war, lead me to performing work as worship.' "But in the business world, a strong emphasis is placed on winning. My boss, Raja, thinks that nothing is more important."

"Winning and competition are linked," replied Yogi. "Both compare others with you, and are dependent on results that are often measured in monetary terms. Concepts like winning and losing are for children who play games. Those with mature minds and awakened Intellects have a more holistic approach to work. They take into consideration not just results, but also righteousness. Work is done not to defeat others, but to improve oneself and to make worthy contributions. As for winning, **victory is there where righteousness is.**"[84]

"What about strategies of war, such as those in *The Art of War*?" I asked.

"One who is in the military or the government should be familiar with the strategies of war," replied Yogi. "They should read books like *The Art of War* and study great Sanskrit texts such as the Mahabharata and *Arthashastra*. They will find useful information on economics, policy, and the military sciences in these texts. The *Arthashastra* preserves the strategies of the Maurya Empire, which covered most of the South Asian subcontinent. It was written by Chanakya, the teacher and minister of Chandragupta Maurya, who founded the empire."

"I remember," I added, recalling my history lessons. "It was his grandson Ashoka the Great who spread Buddhism across all of Asia more than two thousand years before my time."

"Correct," replied Yogi. "Those in the military and government should read these texts from the perspectives of war and governance. Those in the business world can also benefit from these texts, if they study them from the perspectives of business, management, and leadership. However, business persons should be mindful that they are participating in business, not war."

"A valid distinction," I replied in agreement.

"Most humans in some form or another have conflicts, both within themselves and with other humans," added Yogi. "You could consider this conflict to be a war, within the human and external to the human. Some are drawn toward righteousness, light, wisdom, and purity. Others are drawn toward the opposite. Most are drawn in both directions. Those who choose to align themselves in this war with the side of righteousness and light, are advised to use the sword of knowledge and to take refuge in Yoga."

The Gita verse that Yogi was referring to entered my mind.

Therefore, cutting with the sword of knowledge, this doubt about the Atma, born of ignorance, residing in thy heart, take refuge in Yoga. Arise, O Bharata [Prince Arjuna]!
—Lord Krishna in the Bhagavad Gita, 4.42

"The sword of knowledge is not a sword made of metal or other forms of matter," added Yogi. "It is not used for harming the physical bodies of other beings. It is a subtle sword of knowledge and light, used for illumination and peace. It will lead the wielder from darkness to light, and from ignorance to knowledge and wisdom. In the war between light and darkness, take refuge in Yoga. Think of Yoga as a weapon of light. It is a powerful weapon."

I too was in conflict and at war within myself. This was the cause of my crisis. Through Yogi's explanation of Yoga-Vedanta concepts, I was starting to dispel much of the darkness of my ignorance. Things were a lot clearer now that I had been given this weapon of light.

"In total, you have learned four Yogas," continued Yogi. "You will benefit greatly if you practice a holistic blend of all four paths. Now understand this new analogy. Think of the Atma as a bird. This bird has been encaged in a cage made out of ignorance and inaction. The bird can get freedom from the cage by being engaged in the practice of the four Yogas. The bird can take flight by using the two wings of knowledge (Jnana-Yoga) and action (Karma-Yoga). And it can navigate its flight by using the tail feathers of meditation (Raja-Yoga) and devotion (Bhakti-Yoga). Meditation guides knowledge, while devotion guides action. Think of this analogy along with Yoga as a weapon of light and create an image that will help people practice a holistic blend of the four Yogas."

After several moments of thought, I devised a new model. The practice of each Yoga leads to a rise in consciousness. Through the Yoga of Knowledge, we are led from knowledge to wisdom. Through the Yoga of Action, work is transformed into service. When combined, the four Yogas become the Yogas of Wisdom, Meditation, Devotion, and Service (WMDS). The Yogas bring humanity together, build bridges within society, enable the rise in human consciousness, help purify the environment, and bring peace to all beings on Earth. Yoga thus becomes a weapon of light and peace, an alternative to the weapons of mass destruction (WMDs) that have posed a great threat to all life on Earth.

I built the symbol of the four Yogas on the peace sign. It also symbolized a bird, with wisdom and service for the wings and meditation and devotion for the tail to help steer and balance the bird. The ratio of the four Yogas indicate that although all four should be practiced, wisdom and service need to be practiced more if there is to be a balanced contribution toward the individual, society, and all living beings on Earth.

Four Yogas of Wisdom, Meditation, Devotion, and Service

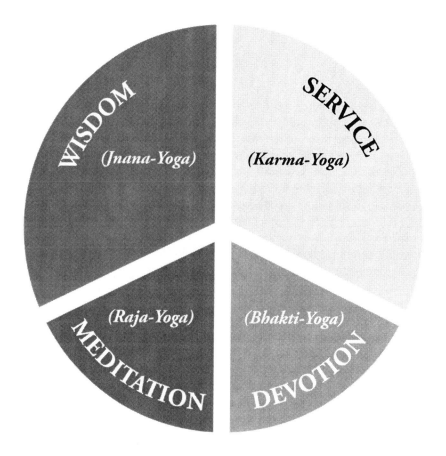

I explained the model to Yogi, who was pleased to see a model that explained a holistic blend of the four Yogas. The flock of swans returned from the lake. They spent a few moments playing with the dog and walked around Yogi and me. After a few moments, they took flight and soared through the air. I watched as they vanished into the sky.

"There is something you must see before you return to your time," said Yogi.

"Go ahead," I replied.

The dog barked and we were covered in golden light. Once the light faded away, I stood up and looked around me. The schools and all inhabitants had disappeared. The lake was much smaller, around a fourth of its original size. The lush green grass had been mostly replaced by dry earth. The trees had mostly disappeared. The dog was still sitting beside us. But there were no swans, lotuses, deer, bees, or other living organisms. The mountains, however, still stood.

"Where are we?" I asked.

"Same place," replied Yogi.

"When?"

"On the day we met."

"What happened to the forest?"

"The trees were cut to produce furniture and firewood. When the forest disappeared, so did the animals, birds, and insects that lived in the forest."

"What happened to the schools, the teachers, students, and sages?"

"Over the centuries, the balance between the four values—Dharma, wealth, pleasure, and *moksha*—was broken. Dharma and *moksha* fell as society placed more value upon pleasure and wealth. The values of Dharma and *moksha*, being more subtle, are hard to quantify in monetary terms. Humans forgot a simple concept: **not all that is of value can be quantified in monetary terms.** This resulted in a reduction in the number of people teaching, studying, and practicing the values of Dharma and *moksha*. Once common in ancient South Asia, schools like the one you saw have vanished with time."

I took another look at my surroundings.

"You have made your point," I said.

"Humans need to stop living in denial," Yogi added. "They are facing a tremendous crisis. They need to start accepting that they are adversely affecting the Earth. Once they do that, they can adopt more balanced and sustainable ways. You are good at mathematics. The population of the Earth's human species surpassed seven billion in your time. The process of deforestation is being repeated across the globe. Do a projection in your mind based on this trend and envision a world without forests and trees. What will happen when there are too many humans and too few trees and other life forms?"

"One does not need to do much math to discern that the ways of humans are not sustainable. If we do an extrapolation of these trends, there is only one logical conclusion—extinction. First, the extinction of the innocents—the tigers, whales, and other endangered or threatened species. Eventually, this will lead to the extinction of the species that is the root cause of the crisis—the human species."

"What can avert this?"

"The trend must change. A turning point must be reached in the consciousness of humans. The collective human consciousness must rise. As for managers, they need to consider the environmental impact of every decision. Let us return to the ancient forest."

The dog barked and we were once again transported through golden light into the past.

"True wisdom leads to living in harmony with the Earth and all life on Earth," Yogi said, repeating his advice. "Everything springs from the earth and everything, when destroyed, merges with the Earth. The Earth is the stay and refuge of all creatures and the Earth is eternal.[85] Great will be the merit earned by the person who will liberate from the meshes of death the whole Earth, with her elephants, vehicles, and horses, overwhelmed with a dreadful calamity.[86] Swami Vivekananda spoke along similar lines."

I recalled sections of the Swami's speeches.

"First, we have to bear in mind that we are all debtors to the world and the world does not owe us anything. It is a great privilege for all of us to be allowed to do anything for the world. In helping the world we really help ourselves."

"If the world is created for us, we are also created for the world. That this world is created for our enjoyment is the most wicked idea that holds us down. This world is not for our sake. Millions pass out of it every year; the world does not feel it; millions of others are supplied in their place. Just as much as the world is for us, so we also are for the world."

—Swami Vivekananda[87]

Considering these thoughts, I added two new principles to my list of Yogic Management principles.

Practice a holistic blend of the four Yogas of wisdom, meditation, devotion, and service.

Always take into consideration the environmental implications of all your actions in work and in life. True wisdom leads to living in harmony with the Earth and all life on Earth.

I also added two new lines to the Yogic Management Mantra.

From being encaged in ignorance, lead me to being engaged in wisdom, meditation, devotion, and service.

From thinking the Earth exists for humans, lead me to understand that humans cannot exist without the Earth.

"When you return to your time, remember that you are more than a manager," Yogi continued. "You are an advisor. An advisor has great responsibilities that cannot be taken lightly. Poison slays only one person, and a weapon also only one. Bad counsel, however, destroys an entire

133

kingdom with king and subject.[88] Insincere persons, who speak sweet and pleasant words, are common on this Earth. But those who speak unpleasant yet beneficial words, as well as those who are open to hearing such words, are very rare. A true advisor is one who, disregarding what is pleasant and unpleasant, gives that advice that may be unpleasant yet beneficial, like bitter medicine."[89]

"I will remember that," I replied.

"You have asked me many questions since we met. I will now ask you some questions to see if you have been attentive."

"Please proceed."

15. Principles of Yogic Management

"What is fleeter than the wind?" asked Yogi.[90]
"The mind is fleeter than the wind," I answered.
"And what is more numerous than grass?"
"Our thoughts are more numerous than grass."
"What is the most valuable of all possessions?"
"The best of all possessions is knowledge."
"What is the best of all kinds of happiness?"
"Contentment is the best of all kinds of happiness."
"What is the highest Dharma?"
"Non-injury is the highest Dharma."
"With what is the world enveloped?"
"The world is enveloped with ignorance."
"What is that because of which a thing cannot be discovered?"
"It is ignorance that does not permit a thing to show itself."
"What is ignorance?"
"True ignorance is to not know one's duties."
"What is idleness?"
"To not discharge one's duties is idleness."
"What also is a true bath?"
"A true bath is washing the mind clean of all impurities."
"What is charity?"
"Charity is protecting all creatures."
"Who should be regarded as learned?"
"One is to be called learned who knows one's duties."
"You have been attentive," said Yogi, with a smile. "Now, please review for me the principles you've compiled during our discussions."
I located and read the list of Yogic Management principles I had developed:

Principles of Yogic Management

1. Through meditation and intuition, use your mind as a sixth sense to access the infinite library of the universe
2. Mature your mind and awaken your Intellect by cultivating wisdom and expanding your consciousness
3. Channel the fire of your mind toward illumination, not toward ignorance or destruction
4. Achieve guaranteed success by performing work for the sake of the work and not for the results of the work. Let the ends and the means be joined as one by treating your work as the ends as well as the means to the end
5. Practicing non-attachment to the fruits (results) of work, focus on what you can influence, on your contributions, knowledge, and actions. Do not get distracted and waste your energy worrying about future outcomes that are not completely under your influence
6. Make decisions with a pure motive and then perform actions with a positive mind and by using proper means
7. Live a balanced lifestyle by being balanced in work, relaxation, recreation, and all other activities
8. Always treat people equally. Never discriminate against anybody based on their gender, race, ethnicity, religion, age, or any other criteria
9. Fill your mind with positive, pure, and righteous thoughts, which you put into practice in words, spoken or written, and in deeds performed. Establish your character by always practicing good thoughts, words, and deeds
10. Make character the most important criteria you use when you hire employees. A position is never wasted if it is assigned to the good and righteous
11. Derive strength from your Atma, the source of tremendous light and energy that resides within your body's five sheaths. Don't limit your potential for greatness by relying on praise or competition from external sources for your motivation
12. Understand that true education teaches humility and builds character, which leads to wealth, Dharma and happiness
13. Pursue education and wealth as if you were to live forever. Practice Dharma as if you were to die at any moment
14. Live a purposeful life by living an L-shaped or U-shaped life
15. Always consider Dharma (righteousness, duty) above wealth (income, savings) and wealth above pleasure (expenses, consumption)

16. Establish Dharma in the world of business by practicing Yogic Management
17. Practice a holistic blend of the four Yogas of wisdom, meditation, devotion, and service
18. Always take into consideration the environmental implications of all your actions in work and in life. True wisdom leads to living in harmony with the Earth and all life on Earth

"Are there any other questions you have for me?" asked Yogi.

"I cannot think of any more at this moment," I replied.

"Then I will leave you with the three verses that are among the last verses spoken by Lord Krishna in the Bhagavad Gita."

The Lord, O Arjuna, dwells in the hearts of all beings, causing all beings, by His Maya [illusion], to revolve, (as if) mounted on a machine.
Take refuge in Him with all thy heart, O Bharata [Prince Arjuna]; by His grace shalt thou attain supreme peace (and) the eternal abode.
Thus has wisdom more profound than all profundities, been declared to thee by Me; reflecting over it fully, act as thou likest.
—Lord Krishna in the Bhagavad Gita, 18.61 to 63

"Notice what the Lord says in the last verse," added Yogi. "After giving Prince Arjuna these divine teachings, the Lord tells him to think holistically by reflecting on the teachings as a whole and to then do as he wishes. The choice of what to do next is Prince Arjuna's. You too must think holistically and do as you wish."

"I have reflected on your teachings holistically," I replied. "I will contribute toward the purpose of establishing Dharma by building the bridge of knowledge between Yoga-Vedanta and Management. Thank you for being my guru and for dispelling my ignorance."

"Namaste," said Yogi, with folded palms while bowing his head down slightly. "**May you <u>always</u> be successful.**"

"Namaste," I replied.

"Woof!" barked the dog.

"Namaste," I said to the dog.

I was then covered again with golden light and transported through time and space.

16. "You're Fired"

As the golden light disintegrated, I took a look around to see where I was. I was back at the park in Gurgaon, sitting on the same bench where I first met Yogi. I glanced at my watch. It still showed 6:19 a.m., but it was ticking again. The corresponding verse entered my mind.

'As a lamp in a spot sheltered from the wind does not flicker,' – even such has been the simile used for a Yogi of subdued mind, practising concentration in the Self.
—Lord Krishna in the Bhagavad Gita, 6.19

I used my Intellect to calm my mind and took a few deep breaths. I also remembered a Yogic Management principle: channel the fire of your mind toward illumination, not toward ignorance or destruction.

I got up and proceeded to Characterra. When I got to my desk, I reviewed the presentation slides for the new chemical factory to be constructed in a tribal region in India. The presentation to the clients was scheduled for 8:30 a.m. The plan was for Raja to make some opening remarks and introduce the Characterra team. After that, I was to deliver the presentation and recommend Option 4, which involved disposing waste into a neighboring river and two lakes. The presentation had to change. I revised it to make Option 1 the recommended option because it had good returns on investment, and also did not cause any known risks to people or the environment.

A few minutes remained before the presentation. I glanced at my cufflinks to see the Ace of Spades and King of Hearts. I remembered Raja's words: "It means that I am a king and always have an ace up my sleeve." And I also remembered his equation for the winning score in blackjack.

K + A = 21

Clearly my conversations with Yogi had changed my thinking. I no longer saw what Raja saw. All I could see in the cufflinks was the Knowledge Work Equation.

K + A = R

Knowledge (*jnana*) + Action (*karma*) = Results (*karma-phala*)

The King of Hearts reminded me to get my knowledge from within, while the Ace of Spades reminded me to act righteously. I was pleased that I didn't have an "R" cufflink; looking down only at the "K" and "A" was a good reminder to stay focused on the LHS of the equation—on my knowledge and actions—while remaining non-attached to the results of work.

I decided to keep the cufflinks. The watch, however, was starting to feel heavy on my wrist. I released myself of the burden and put the watch back into the box it came in. I left it on my desk, next to my name plate that read "Arjun Atmanand, Associate Partner." Intuitively, I perceived that I would no longer need the watch or the name plate.

Raja walked into my office a few minutes before the presentation.

"They are here," he said, referring to the clients. "Ready for battle?"

"I am ready," I replied, and then walked with him to the boardroom.

We met the client, Maya Lobha. She was around forty years old and had recently inherited the leadership of a large family owned conglomerate after the death of her father. This was her third engagement with Characterra. She had been extremely pleased with the prior two engagements in which Raja had made her a lot of money. Both situations had involved Raja working his magic with the authorities. Now, Maya was in a good mood as Raja had already informed her about how lucrative Option 4 would be.

There were quite a few people in the boardroom; eleven from Characterra and seven representing Maya and her team. Raja spent the first ten minutes giving a very smooth sales pitch. He praised Maya and her conglomerate, and stated that he saw them becoming a global powerhouse. He also stressed how strong their partnership with Characterra had grown and how it would continue to grow. Maya praised Raja in return, calling him the smartest person she had ever done business with. After both their egos had been stroked, Raja let me proceed with the presentation.

The presentation fared much as the stock market did during the global financial crisis. It started on a high note, after Raja had inflated the client's expectations into a bubble of hot air. But within two minutes, I had burst the bubble and recommended Option 1. I mentioned Options 2 and 3 as alternate scenarios I had analyzed, but Maya had clearly been expecting to hear something else.

Maya gave Raja a sharp look and asked me about Option 4. I stated that it was neither presented nor recommended because of the risks. I explained that the risks included reputational risk for Maya and probable legal ramifications in the long run. In addition, the health and environmental hazards needed to be factored in. Overall, I recommended a strategic approach that would lead to sustainable results in the long term. But Raja and Maya were only interested in short term gains and making the highest returns possible within the lowest amount of investment and time. Very quickly, Maya's good mood changed into disappointment followed by anger. Raja intervened by cutting the meeting short and stating that there had been some communication errors on Characterra's end. He explained that Characterra had just had a massive reorganization and blamed the terminated staff for the confusion that caused these errors. He also promised that he would resolve all the issues himself and reschedule the presentation for the very next day. Reassured, Maya calmed down a bit and left the Characterra premises with her team. As soon as they had left, Raja's calmness was replaced by anger and frustration. We were now in the hallway and most people on the floor could hear the battle of words that followed.

"What the hell was that?" Raja shouted at me. "You have put me in a very difficult situation. I'm going to have to do some serious damage control now. I demand an explanation."

"Option 1 is the best option for the client and Characterra," I replied. "It is my duty to advise our clients to do what is in their best interests."

"Your duty is to follow my orders."

"My duty is to perform work that benefits Characterra, its clients, and all who are impacted in the process. And when your orders are in conflict with what benefits the stakeholders, it becomes my duty as an advisor to recommend that you reconsider your orders."

"You will advise me to change my orders?"

"If needed, yes. We should not be giving our clients advice that gives them short term gains at the cost of long term risks just because it is in our best short term interest to do so. Profits are important, but not at the cost of principles. Results are important, but not at the cost of righteousness."

Raja shook his head in disbelief and sighed heavily while pacing a few steps up and down the hallway.

"You are my supreme student," he said. "I have invested a lot to make you the warrior that you are today. I even promised to make you a king. But now it appears that my years of mentorship have been wasted. Why are you standing here and spouting mumbo jumbo? Is this the way to repay your teacher who has taught you everything you know? Why are you doing this to me?"

"I am doing this for you, and for Characterra and its clients," I replied calmly. "The option that you wanted me to recommend would have caused harm not just to the environment and society, but also to our client, Characterra, and you. I recommended the most lucrative option that would not cause injury to others."

"Enough of this nonsense about duty and non-injury. Have you not learned anything from history? Mahatma Gandhi personified non-injury. He lived his life doing good and fought for the benefit of others. What did he get in return? How was Martin Luther King, Jr. rewarded for his service to humanity? See a trend? Extrapolate on it! It is stupid to do good for others when others do not reciprocate your goodness."

He sighed some more and then changed his tone. He started acting like something was wrong with me and that he was concerned about my wellbeing.

"Never mind," he said, now calmly. "All is not lost. I will cook up some story and get us out of this mess. You are having a personal crisis. It happens sometimes when one is subjected to a lot of stress. You have worked long hours and have not taken a break. I can see that you have not been sleeping well. What you need is a nice vacation. I will arrange for it. Once you have had a few nights of deep sleep, you will be yourself again."

"I was asleep," I replied. "Now I am awake."

"I am very upset today," he said, raising his voice again. "Don't irritate me further with your nonsense. You go home now and get some sleep. I will present Option 4 tomorrow."

"I cannot allow you to present Option 4."

"If you want to sink your career, that is your decision. But do not ever make the mistake of being a bottleneck in my path to greatness. Don't forget that I can replace you as easily as I can snap my fingers. There are many people more experienced and educated than you who will be honored to have the privilege of working for me. Your vacation has just started. You can decide if you want it to be temporary or permanent."

"Understood. But, as long as I am advisor to our clients and you, it is my duty to advise you against decisions that can cause harm to Characterra, its clients, and other stakeholders."

"Then you leave me with no choice. I relieve you of your duties. You're fired! You are finished in this business. When you apply for jobs, give my name as a reference. I will let people know what an unreliable, ungrateful loser you are."

Raja then pointed at a security guard.

"You," he shouted. "Come here and escort this ignorant fool out of the building. And make sure that he never steps into Characterra ever again. Albert! Where's Albert?"

"You fired him yesterday," I said.

"Yes, he was another loser. Whoever is now in charge of IT support, make sure that you disable all of Arjun's accounts immediately. He must not be able to access any of the knowledge on our hard drives and books."

As I was being escorted out by the security guard, I remembered the conversation I had with Raja the day I first met him, when he interviewed me for an opening at Characterra. I had said that I did not know what wisdom was and had dismissed the term as a buzzword that was fancy sounding but lacking in substance. In response Raja had laughed and said that he also did not know what wisdom was. I turned around to say a few last words to him.

"Raja," I said. "Characterra is not a factory from the Industrial Age, in which the owners owned the machines and other tools of production. It is a consulting firm of the Knowledge Age. Hard drives and books contain only data and information. Knowledge and wisdom exist within the human being, and the most important tool of production in the Knowledge Age is the human mind. When employees leave an organization, they take with them their knowledge and wisdom. Executives must value their employees as their most valuable assets, for when the employees are lost, their knowledge and wisdom are also lost. The biggest loser in the corporate world is an executive who consistently loses good employees. Sadly, you don't know the value of your employees or the difference between information and knowledge. As for wisdom, as on the day we first met, you still don't know what wisdom is."

A quick elevator ride later, I found myself at the entrance of the building in which I had spent most of my waking hours over the last eight years. From the road, I took a long last look at the ivory-colored tower. As I turned around, my attention fell upon the beggar stationed on the other side of the road. He did not look like an insect, as Raja had described him. In fact, unlike an insect with many legs, this beggar had no legs. In spite of all his misfortunes, the beggar looked at me and smiled. I returned his smile.

It was around 9:00 a.m. and the road was packed with traffic. It felt strange having no job to go to. But, I felt like a great burden had been lifted from my shoulders, just as Atlas from Greek mythology would have felt if he released the Earth he was carrying. I decided to wander around and explore the city.

I spent the morning and afternoon wandering around. When I went home, I relaxed some more. At around 8:00 p.m., I started feeling very tired and sleepy. Years of an imbalanced lifestyle and poor sleep habits had caught up to me. I went to bed and had the deepest, most relaxing sleep I had ever had. That was the last time I had any of my recurring dreams.

It was the dream in which I was running around in circles on a road made of reddish-brown earth. Many people from my life, including Karan and Raja, were running with me, all dressed in red. The dream was the same as before, until the point where Karan and I stop running.

"Don't stop," Karan said. "Continue running."

I looked up and saw the finishing point, marked by a red banner, which was on top of a nearby hill. Yogi and the dog were standing by the banner, along with Swami Vivekananda, Swami Sivananda, and many other yogis. Raja and my colleagues had also stopped running and were now gathered around Karan and me. I paused and then realized something.

"It's time to stop running," I said to Karan. "It's time to rise."

And then I felt light. I was rising above the ground and into the air. I rose to the height of the hill and then moved horizontally till I reached the banner that marked the finishing point. I was greeted with smiles. And then Swami Vivekananda said, "Awake, arise, and dream no more!"

17. The Bridge of Knowledge

I woke up immediately after the Swami's words entered my mind. I glanced at my alarm clock. Once more it showed 4:42 a.m. The corresponding verse entered my mind.

> Therefore, cutting with the sword of knowledge, this doubt about the Atma, born of ignorance, residing in thy heart, take refuge in Yoga. Arise, O Bharata [Prince Arjuna]!
> —Lord Krishna in the Bhagavad Gita, 4.42

I felt refreshed and highly motivated to start a new life. I cleaned up my apartment and installed a desk and chair for my new home office. It was time to build the bridge of knowledge between Yoga-Vedanta and Management. Incredibly, I found the sheets of paper, on which I had put the frameworks and principles of Yogic Management, in the pocket of the suit I was wearing in the park. I started by writing down what I had learned from Yogi and all who I had met through him. I still remembered every verse from the Gita that I had gained through intuition. I also started doing additional research on Yoga and Vedanta by reading the other great texts, including the Upanishads, Yoga Sutras, and Mahabharata. Yogi had also advised me that intellectual nutrition, like food, is most beneficial when taken closer to the source. I hence chose to read the texts themselves instead of the interpretations of other scholars.

I also researched to see if there were people in the past who had set standards we could follow. I learned about Andrew Carnegie, whose life was a rags-to-riches story and a great source of inspiration. Unfortunately, most students or practitioners of Management have never heard of him. He was an American industrialist who made a fortune in the steel industry in the nineteenth century. Adjusted for inflation, his wealth was the second highest of any person in modern history, second only to John D. Rockefeller. He was also one of the world's greatest philanthropists. By the time of his death, he had donated most of his wealth to worthy causes, including educational institutions, libraries, and music halls that continue to contribute to society in the twenty-first century.

The following is an excerpt from Andrew Carnegie's essay, The Gospel of Wealth, written in 1889. I believe that this essay should be read by all practicing managers and taught at all business schools.

"This, then, is held to be the **duty** of the man of **wealth**: To set an example of modest, unostentatious living, shunning display or extravagance; to provide moderately for the legitimate wants of those dependent upon him; and, after doing so, to consider all surplus revenues which come to him simply as trust funds, which he is called upon to administer, and strictly bound as a matter of **duty** to administer in the manner which, in his **judgment**, is best calculated to produce the most beneficial results for the community—the man of wealth thus becoming the mere trustee and agent for his poorer brethren, bringing to their **service** his superior **wisdom**, experience, and ability to administer, doing for them better than they would or could do for themselves."
—Andrew Carnegie

Over a hundred years after he wrote this paragraph, I could not have written it with greater clarity, or used a better choice of words—duty (Dharma), wealth (*artha*), judgment (*viveka*, discernment), service (Karma-Yoga) and wisdom (*vijnana*).

Carnegie's dictum was:
   • to spend the first third of one's life getting all the education one can,
   • to spend the next third making all the money one can, and
   • to spend the last third giving it all away for worthwhile causes.

His dictum encompassed the first three of four phases in the Purposeful Life Framework. His life was a perfect example of an L-shaped life. It is my hope that more of the world's wealthiest people will be inspired by Carnegie to progress from the professional phase to the philanthropist phase. I am reminded of the following verse.

Whatsoever the superior person does, that is followed by others. What he demonstrates by action, that, people follow.
—Lord Krishna in the Bhagavad Gita, 3.21

In addition to research and writing, I started living a balanced life and practicing a holistic blend of the four Yogas. Through breathing exercises, postures, and meditation, I became healthier than I had ever been in my life. In addition, I changed my diet and noticed that I gained more energy and mental alertness, which helped improve my productivity in knowledge work. I minimized my intake of canned and processed food, avoided all fast foods and soft drinks, reduced my sugar consumption, and gave up second hand sources of nutrition, including meat. I educated myself on which

145

foods offered what kinds of nutrition, and learned how to cook them to maximize the freshness and nutritional content. I also started to strengthen my diet by taking supplements, including my two favorites, Chyawanprash and Spirulina. Chyawanprash is a paste made of herbs and other healthy ingredients recommended in Ayurveda, the traditional medicine of India. Spirulina is a unicellular algae that is an excellent source of protein and other nutrients. It was harvested and consumed by the Aztecs and other native people of the Americas. I believe that anyone can gain improved physical and mental health through the right diet and the practice of yogic breathing, postures, and meditation.

Around three months after I was fired from Characterra, some interesting news started to spread about the firm's client, Maya Lobha. Environmental activists had learned about the environmental hazards being caused by Lobha's conglomerate. Lawsuits were filed for a variety of their activities, the most prominent of which were the two previous and one current project for which they were advised by Characterra. The legal system proceeded slowly with these cases. But the media and citizens were quick to react. Journalists and bloggers performed their duty as the "senses" of society and reported extensively on the environmental and health hazards. Through social media, citizens across the country mobilized and pledged to boycott all products produced by Lobha's companies. Consumers started to think of their money as votes. Every unit of currency spent was a vote of confidence in a particular product or company, which led to the future success of that product or company. Any product or company that was boycotted by a sufficient number of consumers would eventually fail.

Initially, Maya Lobha was arrogant, publicly dismissing the charges along with her entourage of highly paid lawyers. Within weeks, the revenues earned by her companies were decimated. She borrowed heavily to maintain the status quo. Within three months of the first lawsuit, she had to default on her loans and declare bankruptcy, losing her companies as well as her homes and other personal belongings. In her final press release, reduced to poverty and abandoned by her lawyers, she apologized and declared that her mind had been poisoned by the bad advice of Raja Sahamkar.

Raja, in turn, was abandoned by his clients. Most of his clients and many of his employees quickly moved to a new consulting firm named Khan and Pandit Consulting. I learned that the two professors, Payal Khan (Professor Pi) and Abhay Pandit, had approached their former employers, Singh and Patel. Singh and Patel provided the funding required for the professors to start their own consulting firm. All the other employees who had been let go by Characterra, and had worked previously for Singh and Patel, were hired by Khan and Pandit Consulting.

Much to my surprise, I was approached by the professors soon after this new consulting firm was formed and was offered a job, in spite of the role I had played in firing them from Characterra. The professors had heard about my altercation with Raja and the circumstances of my dismissal. I politely declined their offer and mentioned that I wanted to focus on my research and writing. Once my book was published, the professors hired me as an independent consultant at a very generous hourly rate. I served as "advisor of advisors," advising the consultants and clients using Yogic Management. I spent around two days a week on consulting engagements, and the rest on my research and writing. This balance between practice and theory worked well for me.

As for Raja, the last I had heard was that he shut down Characterra soon after he lost his clients. He was working on his next venture, but nobody knew the details.

My writings started out as separate *rudraksha* beads, individual diagrams and charts I had sketched while conversing with Yogi. Over the span of few months, they started connecting with each other to form a chain of beads. As the individual sections of writing came together, the book was completed and ready for publication. Publication was made easier by a new phenomenon in the publishing industry, the rise of the electronic book (ebook). This medium had a great appeal to me because of the speed and efficiency with which my writings could be shared with a global audience and by the fact that ebooks minimize the impact on the environment. This medium was also effective because of the growing global popularity of tablets and electronic book readers. In addition to the ebook, I made the book available in the form of paperbacks since there are many people who still prefer to read books on paper instead of electronic devices.

The next challenge was to get the word out and make people aware of the book. This is never easy for a first time author who nobody knows about. I did what I could by using social media tools such as videos, blogs, and networking sites. In addition, I started submitting articles to magazines and media organizations that would find my writings to be of interest. As awareness grew, people started to read the book. Soon, I started to get called to give talks at bookstores and at various alumni and professional organizations. It was fulfilling to interact with those who had read the book and were applying the principles and frameworks of Yogic Management to their work and life.

At one such event at a bookstore, the store manager requested me to stay back to sign books. I signed each one with the same message: "May you always be successful."

"Name?" I asked, as I got to the last person waiting for a signed copy.

"Jyoti," a woman replied, in a voice I had heard before.

It was Jyoti Ramasethu, the counselor I had met the year before for a session on handling stress. I said goodbye to the event organizers and walked out with Jyoti.

"Have you read the book?" I asked.

"Yes," she replied, with a smile. "Clearly, you have found ways to deal with your stress."

"I did find some answers," I added, with a laugh.

"You definitely did. What are you working on these days?"

"In addition to events like these, I am doing research for a second book that I wish to publish."

"Have you considered including the field of psychology into your research? Management has already incorporated many concepts from psychology."

I had not considered this, though Jyoti made a valid point. Psychologists study the mind, and I had redefined Management for the Knowledge Age to be mind (*man*) maturity (agement). Psychology would definitely be a field that could lead to advances in Yogic Management.

"That's a great suggestion," I replied. "Would you be interested in collaborating on my research?"

"Yes. You still have nine one-hour sessions with me remaining," she replied with a laugh.

"Excellent. Another bridge can be built."

"It can. By the way, I'm curious to know how you found your answers."

"It's an extraordinary story. If I tell you, you might think I have lost my mind."

"I like extraordinary stories."

"I thought you told me you liked to hear the ordinary story of each person's life the best," I said. We laughed.

"It's my opinion that everyone's story is extraordinary." She looked at me with one eyebrow arched. "But I have a feeling the story you are about to tell me is more extraordinary than most."

"Well, there are two versions to it. The short version is that one day, on my way to work, I stopped at a park to spend some time *with my Self*," I said, and then asked the question I wanted to ask her many months ago. "How about I tell you the long version of the story over a coffee?"

"Sounds good."

We exchanged phone numbers. This time I called her. We met for a coffee—the first of many to come.

18. You May Say I'm a Dreamer

Eleven months had gone by since I had met Yogi. I was scheduled to give an evening workshop on Yogic Management. It was set up by a firm that organizes events and invites motivational speakers. There were over a hundred people in the audience, including a special guest. My brother Karan had just flown in from New York on a business trip and had decided to attend the event. After the event, I joined him for dinner at an upscale restaurant in the hotel where he was staying.

"Good workshop," Karan said. "You make an excellent motivational speaker and I was impressed by the way you handled the questions."

"Thanks," I replied.

"You seem happy with what you are doing. Are you making much money in the process?"

"I'm making money through my consulting and speaking engagements, and royalties from my book."

"Are you making as much as you were making before?"

"The amount is not so important to me. I'm living a life of purpose and am content with whatever rewards the universe may grant me. In addition, I have gained fulfillment from my work, a wonderful feeling that is hard to quantify. Not all that is of value can be quantified in monetary terms."

"Artists are also happy with what they do. But most end up becoming starving artists. For every four who become the Beatles, there are millions who make a living as waiters and retail store clerks. Give what you are doing another six months. If by then you can't match your previous income, you may want to consider getting a real job. Every venture must first have an exit strategy. Anyway, I'm glad to see you happy."

"How are things with you?"

"Things are going really well. My fund has been immensely successful over the last year. Many high net worth clients signed up with me on my last trip and more are interested in investing with me. Check this out."

Karan gave me a brochure of his fund.

"I'm now offering more sophisticated derivatives," he continued. "These give my investors higher returns at lower risks."

"This is very impressive, Karan," I said after reviewing his brochure. "I am confident that you will give your clients excellent returns, while earning several millions of dollars in fees. I have some questions, though."

"Go ahead."

"You are not producing anything. What you are doing is using your mathematical and financial expertise to redistribute a finite sum of money owned by a finite number of people. In the process, your high net worth clients will become even richer, while the other smaller investors lose their investments and become poorer. What value do you or your investment banking peers on Wall Street bring to society or the environment?"

"This is the way the system works. It is capitalism at its finest. I bring value to my clients and become rich in the process."

"Correct. You make the rich richer, the poor poorer, and destroy the middle class—the backbone of every nation's economy. It is people like you who've created the financial crisis that started in 2008 and caused great misery around the globe. Your work doesn't add any value to society, the environment, or anything that matters. Wall Street builds walls and divides society between the extremely rich and the extremely poor. We don't need walls. We need bridges. The fact is, you are part of the problem that has put humanity and all life on Earth in a state of great crisis. Instead, you could have been a part of the solution."

"What are you accusing me of?" asked Karan, getting defensive.

"Greed, insatiable greed."

Karan argued with me for several minutes to justify the importance of his work. But he was intelligent, and deep inside knew that I made a valid point that his profession did not add much value to society or the environment. The harm he was doing in the process, however, seemed to be something he was previously unaware of.

At one point, the music playing at the restaurant changed to John Lennon's "Imagine."

"Arjun," Karan said, with a smile. "You are a dreamer."

"Sometimes I dream," I replied. "But let's focus for a moment on you. Do you acknowledge that there are many problems facing society, the environment, and all life on Earth?"

"Yes."

"You acknowledge the problems, yet you use your knowledge and skills to exploit the system to your advantage. You choose to be a part of the problem, instead of making a difference and being a part of the solution. Would you be interested in being part of the solution?"

"I'm listening."

"You are intelligent, educated, and an expert in mathematics applied to finance. You are good at doing so many things—selling, motivating, raising capital, etc. **Imagine a world in which people who are good at doing things started doing good things.** Imagine that they do so not for name or fame, but just because good will come from it. We are told that we should go from 'good to great' and that good is the enemy of great. But in the pursuit of becoming great, we have forgotten the importance of being good. Great should not be the enemy of good. Greatness can be achieved through goodness. Imagine a world in which people strive to achieve 'greatness through goodness.' How would such a world be?'"

I gave Karan a few seconds to think about this.

"Such a world would indeed be a better world," he said.

"As we speak, a war is taking place between the forces of light and darkness, between righteousness and unrighteousness. It's not a war fought with physical weapons, but with knowledge and wealth. You are fighting for the wrong side, for darkness and unrighteousness."

"I don't know what war you are talking about. And even if there was a war, I am neutral, like Switzerland."

"Behind the facade of neutrality, Switzerland is an agent of darkness, poverty, pain, and suffering."

"I've never heard this logic before. Please explain."

"Switzerland enables corruption by allowing its banks to provide safe haven to corrupt and unrighteous people who are looting the wealth of honest and righteous people. Until the Swiss banks disclose and repatriate these funds to the people who suffered, the Swiss will be unethical warriors of darkness. They are part of the problem with the system. For profits from banking fees, they are taking on the karmic demerit that results from causing pain and suffering on Earth."

"Your point is logical," Karan replied, after some thought. "From corruption, millions across the globe live in a state of poverty and suffering. Many have died in the process from starvation, suicide, and disease. They who enable this suffering are as responsible as those who cause it."

"Correct," I added. "You have a great fire within you. The point to note is that this fire can illuminate by creating light or it can destroy by burning things to ashes. You need to focus your fire on worthy and righteous causes. In the Mahabharata, the great warrior Karna fought on the side of unrighteousness against his own brothers. Lord Krishna advised him not to, but he still did and eventually perished. Don't be like Karna. I have an idea for you. Have you considered doing business with the world's poorest people? Perhaps you could consider social entrepreneurship? You could fund ventures and innovations that create social change."

"I work with high net worth individuals. How can you help those who are at the bottom of the pyramid and have no resources with which they can help themselves?"

"What pyramid are you referring to?"

"A wealth pyramid, with the poorest at the bottom layer and the richest at the top layer."

"Is wealth the only resource? Isn't knowledge also a resource in the Knowledge Age?"

"Yes," Karan replied, after thinking for a few seconds. "I see where you are going. Knowledge is a resource."

"The poor may be at the bottom of the wealth pyramid," I said. "But in terms of knowledge, wisdom, values, and ethics, they can be more advanced than many bankers and politicians. Because they are poor, they are frugal and waste less of the Earth's resources. They find ways to make do with whatever little they can afford. They may not have capital and wealth. But they have knowledge, ingenuity, and resourcefulness, built upon generations of having to innovate and meet their needs while faced with scarcity of resources. Each year, inventions and innovations are created by the poor that greatly improve the condition of human beings across the world. And because many live in rural areas, they are in touch with nature and have not forgotten how to live in harmony with the Earth and all life on Earth. They are not asking for handouts. What they need is a platform, similar to the one you have already created for your wealthy clients."

"I don't know anything about working with poor people."

"You may not know much today. But you are intelligent, and a mathematical and financial genius. If you apply your mind to it, I am positive you will become an expert. What do you think?"

"It sounds like a challenge worth pursuing."

"Glad to hear that. A Yogic Manager would gladly take on such a challenge."

"'Yogic Manager?'" he exclaimed with a raised eyebrow. "I always thought you would become an investment banker. I never thought of you as an author or teacher. I had hoped that I would convince you to join me in my venture and make us both a lot of money. Instead, you are trying to get me to join you, in some kind of a revolution."

"Not a revolution," I clarified. "In a revolution, only the players are changed. But since the new players share similar thinking as the old players, there is no sustainable improvement to society. It's like a wheel revolving over and over, but stuck at the same spot. Yogic Management is not a *revolution*; it's an *evolution* of Management. By raising the consciousness of managers, it can bring about sustainable improvements to society, environment, and all life on Earth."

"Give me an elevator pitch. You have ninety seconds. Why should I become a Yogic Manager?"

"Yogic Managers are more than just managers. We are the subset of managers that apply the principles of Yoga-Vedanta to do work, not just for results, but for righteousness. We bring prosperity, philanthropy, and peace through results, righteousness, and realization. We apply not just knowledge, but that subset of knowledge that is wisdom. Through mature minds, awakened Intellects, and the power of discernment, we strive to do the righteous things righteously. We perform work with pure motives, positive minds, and proper means. Today we are a small percentage of the

Earth's working population. But our numbers are growing. Our growth is directly correlated to the rise in the collective human consciousness. The rise in consciousness feeds our growth in numbers and our growth in turn feeds the rise in human consciousness. One day we will be everywhere—at your work, social gatherings, and various platforms on the internet. You will recognize us by our actions, by the way we think, by the words we speak, and by the deeds we perform. Together we will establish Dharma in the world of business. Together we will elevate the human condition and restore harmony to an imbalanced planet. Together we will lead humanity through the turning point between crisis and consciousness. Would you like to join the evolution of Management?"

Epilogue

The Inspiration

I never dreamed that I would write a book. And I never planned to write this book. It just happened. In 2007, I graduated with an MBA from the Queen's School of Business in Ontario, Canada, and started working at a large Canadian bank in Toronto. Within a year, the financial crisis of 2008 hit the global economy. As I followed the events that unfolded, I started to believe that there was something seriously wrong with the world of business. We value and admire those who think and behave like Raja Sahamkar. But their ways of greed and ignorance are not sustainable. If we continue down the path we are on, bubbles and crises, like the dot-com bubble and the credit crisis, will keep happening. There will be increased suffering to humans and all beings on Earth. We needed an alternative way of thinking.

I looked for answers in the texts of Yoga-Vedanta. Soon after I read these texts, I became flooded with ideas at the most inconvenient times—while traveling to work, eating, showering, and other mundane activities. For several months, I ignored these ideas. Then one day, I decided to carry a notepad so that I could write down an idea every time I got one. Before I realized it, I had hundreds of pages of ideas that I had scribbled in several such notepads. I also started to get thoughts and images in my dreams. On several occasions, I woke up between 4:00 and 5:00 a.m. to put these onto paper. These images include all the frameworks that you see in this book. I realized that I needed to compile these ideas and frameworks in a book, which is exactly what I did. Working part time on this book, it took around four years of research and writing, or as I like to think of it, four years of recreation and worship, to finish this book.

This book is a modern retelling of the ancient Sanskrit epic, the Mahabharata. It was inspired by this epic and, in particular, the literary gem within this epic, the Bhagavad Gita. The inspiration was derived not just for the content and ideas of this book, but also for the format of this book. The Mahabharata makes a magnificent claim in the first of its eighteen books regarding the four values of life:

"Whatever is spoken about Dharma, *artha* (wealth), *kama* (pleasure), and *moksha* (salvation) may be seen elsewhere; but whatever is not contained

154

in this is not to be found anywhere."
—Mahabharata, Book 1, Section 62

These four values or purposes of life have been used as the foundation for the principles and frameworks in this book.

In the Mahabharata, we also find the following analogy at the very beginning of the epic:

"As the sun dispels the darkness, so does the Mahabharata by its discourses on Dharma, *artha*, *kama* and *moksha*, dispel the ignorance of men.

As the full-moon by its mild light expands the buds of the lotus, so this *Purana* (story, epic), by exposing the light of the *Sruti* (scriptures) has expanded the human Intellect. By the lamp of history, which destroys the darkness of ignorance, the whole mansion of nature is properly and completely illuminated."
—Mahabharata, Book 1, Section 1

This book takes the format of the Mahabharata by putting the practices and philosophies of Yoga-Vedanta into the form of stories and characters. The Sanskrit scriptures are like the rays of the sun, which are illuminating, but difficult to look at for an extended period of time. But the epic, which presents the concepts of the scriptures in the form of entertaining stories, is easier to absorb, like moonlight, which can be looked at with ease.

Notes on the Mahabharata

My research in the Mahabharata has convinced me that the epic is a lot deeper than just a mythological story. There are striking parallels between several key characters and important Yoga-Vedanta concepts. I believe that the author, Maharishi Ved Vyasa, was a genius who preserved ancient philosophies in the form of stories by writing about characters who personified various concepts. The Bhagavad Gita, too, is a preservation of these philosophies. When studied in parallel with the Upanishads, it becomes clear that the Gita is a summary of key Yoga-Vedanta concepts presented in the form of a conversation between Lord Krishna and Prince Arjuna. Although a full description of the parallels between characters and concepts is beyond the scope of this book, a brief summary of the story and settings of the Mahabharata and Gita will help clarify how this book adapts the epic.

The central event in the epic is the great war of Kurukshetra fought by the princes of the Kuru dynasty for the throne of Hastinapura. One contender for the throne is the wise, righteous, just, truthful, and moral

King Yudhisthira. The other side fights on behalf of his cousin, the ignorant, unrighteous, greedy, evil, and immoral King Duryodhana. Yudhisthira personifies Dharma, while Duryodhana personifies *adharma*, the opposite of Dharma. The main warrior fighting for Yudhisthira is his younger brother Prince Arjuna. Lord Krishna, the *Avatar* (incarnation on Earth) of Lord Vishnu, participates in the war not as a warrior, but as Arjuna's charioteer. Another great warrior, King Karna, who happens to be the brother of Yudhisthira and Arjuna, chooses to fight, not for his brothers, but for his unrighteous friend Duryodhana. By aligning with unrighteousness, Karna sinks to his demise. Just before the war begins, Prince Arjuna has a moral crisis, caused not out of fear or hate for his opponents, but by his love and respect for those he must fight, including his teacher, relatives, and friends. To help him through his crisis, Lord Krishna, his charioteer, advises him on the battlefield by teaching him about Dharma and related concepts from Yoga and Vedanta. This conversation is the Bhagavad Gita.

The main characters in this book were inspired by important characters in the Mahabharata. The Mahabharata's war of Kurukshetra has been recreated in this book as a war set in the world of business and fought at the management consulting firm, Characterra Consulting. The table below summarizes and links the characters of this book with those in the epic.

Character from this book	Inspiration from the Mahabharata
Arjun Atmanand, an intelligent and hardworking manager and consultant at a consulting firm called Characterra	Prince Arjuna, a powerful warrior who fights on behalf of his righteous brother, King Yudhisthira
Yogi Dharmaraja, an advanced being with supernatural abilities who advises Arjun through his moral crisis	King Yudhisthira, the personification of Dharma and true heir to the throne of Hastinapura
Raja Sahamkar, Arjun's boss, for whom business is war and wealth is more important than ethics	King Duryodhana, the personification of unrighteousness and challenger to the throne
Karan Atmanand, Arjun's brother, who chooses not to use his knowledge and skills for Dharma	King Karna, Prince Arjuna's brother who fights on behalf of King Duryodhana

In this book, Arjun, too, has a moral crisis. The root of his crisis is a conflict between his conscience and the instructions of his boss. The conflict between Arjun Atmanand and Raja Sahamkar symbolizes the conflict between the Atma (soul, true Self) and the *ahamkar* (ego, false self). During his crisis, Arjun is helped by an advanced being with supernatural abilities who calls himself Yogi. Yogi is inspired by the King Yudhisthira, who is often referred to as "Dharmaraja", the righteous king. His dialogues were inspired by the practices and philosophies of Yoga-Vedanta and the words spoken by the Mahabharata's righteous characters, primarily Lord Krishna, Mahatma Vidura and King Yudhisthira. The words spoken by Yogi and Raja that were inspired by the epic have been referenced so that readers may know which book and section of the epic they were taken from.

There are often some challenges in translating ancient concepts into models that make sense and are relevant to modern readers. Depending on the teacher or scholar's interpretation, some of these ancient Yoga-Vedanta concepts can be understood differently. Some readers may not agree with certain aspects of a framework, while others may agree with those aspects but disagree with some other aspects. I request the reader to understand that, while there might be some disagreements about the frameworks, I have done the best I could to represent these ancient concepts in ways that can be applied by modern practitioners of Management.

The (R)Evolution of Management

If you believe as I do that Yogic Management, the bridge between Yoga-Vedanta and Management, is worth strengthening, I request you to join the evolution of Management by visiting my website:
www.yogicmanagement.com

The frameworks (as high resolution charts in full color) and other resources have been made available for free on the website. You will also find more information on the Yogic Management networking group, where you can connect with other Yogic Managers across the globe.

To the professors, researchers and the staff of business schools:
• Please incorporate the Yogic Management principles and frameworks explained in this book as part of your curriculum. These holistic concepts will help develop more mature managers, who will be able to discern between knowledge and wisdom and between results and righteousness. Your schools will become the hubs for a global movement that will elevate the human condition and restore harmony to an imbalanced planet. Through your actions, one day in the future, the discipline of Management will be recognized and respected as the discipline that solved one of the greatest crises faced by humanity.

To Yoga teachers and practitioners:
• Please expand your curriculum and practice to go beyond the postures (*asanas*) and breathing techniques (*pranayama*). Yoga is more than a series of exercises for a healthy body. This ancient practice can help people mature

their minds, awaken their Intellects and realize their Atma. This can happen through a balanced Yoga practice that incorporates the four classic Yogas.

To managers:
• Please practice Yogic Management. You are not merely the managers of money, people, and resources. The future of humanity, the Earth, and all living beings on Earth, depend upon your actions.

To business school students:
• Please share the principles and frameworks of Yogic Management in your discussions, assignments, and presentations. If even one student in a class shares a framework in a presentation to her or his classmates, awareness will rise and ignorance will decline. You can be that student and play an important role in the establishment of Dharma in the world of business.

I wish to conclude this book with the **Yogic Management Mantra**.

From the unreal, lead me to the real,
From darkness, lead me to light,
From mortality, lead me to immortality,
From ignorance, lead me to knowledge,
From knowledge, lead me to wisdom,
From performing work as war, lead me to performing work as worship,
From practicing the art of war, lead me to practicing Yoga, the art of work,
From doing the right things right, lead me to do the righteous thing righteously,
From living an i-shaped life or I-shaped life, lead me to living an L-shaped life or U-shaped life,
From building credit history, lead me to building karmic history,
From being encaged in ignorance, lead me to being engaged in wisdom, meditation, devotion, and service,
From thinking the Earth exists for humans, lead me to understand that humans cannot exist without the Earth.

Acknowledgments

If I have seen further it is only by standing on the shoulders of giants.
—Isaac Newton

Many people contributed toward making this book a reality. I feel a deep sense of gratitude to:

—my mother, Dr. Padmini Sharma, who gave me feedback on multiple versions of this book, and recommended that I write it as a business novel instead of a non-fiction text.

—my father, Dr. Shiv Bhushan Sharma, who introduced me to Yoga at an early age, and designed the images for the seven chakras and *Gita Updesh* used in this book.

—my wife, Simran, who helped with the story, supported my writing with understanding and patience, and always believed in me.

—Dr. Dipak C. Jain, Dean of INSEAD, who contributed the Foreword to this book. I owe him special thanks for taking time from his busy schedule, and sharing his thoughts with all the readers of this book.

—my professors at the Queen's School of Business, who gave me the education I needed to write this book. Thanks in particular to Dr. Tina Dacin and Dr. Jana Raver, for reviewing a draft of this book and giving me their feedback and suggestions.

—Dr. Raj Dubey of the Spiritual Heritage Education Network (SHEN), for reviewing this book, and providing feedback from the perspective of Yoga-Vedanta.

—my editors, Alison Kooistra, Intisar Awisse and Nadiya Osmani; and my designer Nadia Fernando.

—the great teachers of Yoga-Vedanta who set the foundation upon which Yogic Management was built. Thanks in particular to Swami Vivekananda, whose books introduced me to Vedanta, and whose teachings influenced me to practice a holistic blend of the four Yogas. Thanks also to Swami Sivananda and Swami Vishnudevananda, for setting up the International Sivananda Yoga Vedanta Centres, where I learned *asanas* and *pranayama*, growing up in Chennai and many years later in Toronto.

—Peter Drucker, whose books inspired me to study Management.

About the Author

Avinash Bhushan Sharma is a senior consultant for strategic programs at a large Canadian bank in Toronto. He builds business cases, backed by financial models, and advises executives on investment decisions. He earned his MBA from the Queen's School of Business (Ontario), his MS in Computer Science from the New Jersey Institute of Technology (NJIT), and his BSc in Statistics from Loyola College (University of Madras). He is also a graduate of Jiddu Krishnamurti's Rishi Valley School. He previously worked as an analyst at the University of Chicago's National Opinion Research Center (NORC).

Avinash was introduced to Yoga and Indian mythology at an early age by his parents. From 2008 to 2012 he researched Sanskrit texts, including the Mahabharata, Bhagavad Gita, Upanishads, and Yoga Sutras, to determine how Yoga-Vedanta can be applied to Management. The Yogic Manager is the product of this research, and is the first book in the Yogic Management series. To learn more about Yogic Management, and to access a variety of free resources, visit
www.yogicmanagement.com

Notes

[1] Peter Drucker, *The Essential Drucker* 313.

[2] http://en.wiktionary.org/wiki/manage

[3] Bhagavad Gita, Swami Swarupananda (1909); Mahabharata, Kisari Mohan Ganguli (1883-1896); and Upanishads, Swami Nikhilananda.

[4] Inspired by description of *Chakravyuh* in Mahabharata 7.33.

[5] Mahabharata 7.33.

[6] Peter Drucker, *The Effective Executive* 87.

[7] Inspired by Mahabharata 2.48; spoken by King Duryodhana; (Raja does not quote the Mahabharata)

[8] Inspired by Mahabharata 2.54; spoken by King Duryodhana; (Raja does not quote the Mahabharata)

[9] Inspired by Mahabharata 2.54; spoken by King Duryodhana; (Raja does not quote the Mahabharata)

[10] Mahabharata 3.268; spoken by Queen Draupadi, describing King Yudhishthira

[11] Katha Upanishad 1.2.2.

[12] Inspired by the description of a forest in Mahabharata 1.70.

[13] Mahabharata 3.311; spoken by King Yudhishthira

[14] Taittiriya Upanishad 2.1–5 and 3.1–6

[15] Mahabharata 3.134; spoken by Ashtavakra

[16] Inspired by Mahabharata 3.31; spoken by King Yudhishthira

[17] Swami Vivekananda, *Karma Yoga* 2.

[18] Mahabharata 3.311; spoken by King Yudhishthira

[19] Mahabharata 3.4; spoken by Mahatma Vidura

[20] Mahabharata 5.137; spoken by Queen Kunti

[21] Mahabharata 3.295; spoken by Savitri

[22] Mahabharata 3.311; spoken by King Yudhishthira

[23] Mahabharata 3.311; spoken by King Yudhishthira

[24] Mahabharata 2.15; spoken by King Yudhishthira

[25] Bhagavad Gita 13.16.

[26] Mahabharata 5.36; spoken by Mahatma Vidura

[27] Mahabharata 1.115; spoken by Mahatma Vidura

[28] Mahabharata 3.133; spoken by Ashtavakra

[29] Mahabharata 3.311; spoken by King Yudhishthira

[30] Mahabharata 3.199; spoken by Rishi Markandeya

[31] Mahabharata 6.5; spoken by Minister Sanjaya

[32] Inspired by Mahabharata 3.210; spoken by Rishi Markandeya
[33] Inspired by Mahabharata 3.2; spoken by Saunaka
[34] Peter Drucker, *Post-Capitalist Society* 46.
[35] Swami Vivekananda, *Karma Yoga* 1.
[36] Swami Vivekananda, *Karma-Yoga* 8.
[37] Peter Drucker, *Post-Capitalist Society* 46.
[38] Inspired by Mahabharata 2.55; spoken by Rishi Vaisampayana
[39] Mahabharata 1.123; spoken by King Pandu
[40] Mahabharata 5.135; spoken by Queen Kunti
[41] Mahabharata 5.34; spoken by Mahatma Vidura
[42] Mahabharata 1.142; spoken by Minister Kanika
[43] Mahabharata 3.257; spoken by Maharishi Vyasa
[44] Mahabharata 3.311; spoken by King Yudhishthira
[45] Swami Vivekananda, *Karma-Yoga* 63.
[46] Swami Vivekananda, *Karma-Yoga* 39.
[47] Mahabharata 5.35; spoken by Mahatma Vidura
[48] Mahabharata 3.295; spoken by Savitri
[49] Swami Vivekananda, *Karma-Yoga*, 64.
[50] Mahabharata 5.37; spoken by Mahatma Vidura
[51] Inspired by Mahabharata 5.33; spoken by Mahatma Vidura
[52] Mahabharata 3.311; spoken by King Yudhishthira
[53] Swami Vivekananda, *Karma-Yoga* 26.
[54] Mahabharata 5.39; spoken by Mahatma Vidura
[55] Inspired by Mahabharata 3.32; spoken by Queen Draupadi
[56] Mahabharata 5.35; spoken by Mahatma Vidura
[57] Inspired by Mahabharata 2.74; spoken by Queen Gandhari
[58] Mahabharata 3.180; spoken by, King Nahusha
[59] Mahabharata 5.33; spoken by Mahatma Vidura
[60] Mahabharata 5.93; spoken by Lord Krishna
[61] Mahabharata 2.67; spoken by Mahatma Vidura
[62] Inspired by Mahabharata 1.182; spoken by Rishi Aurva
[63] Mahabharata 3.215; spoken by Rishi Markandeya
[64] Swami Vivekananda, *Karma-Yoga* 36.
[65] Mahabharata 3.311; spoken by King Yudhishthira
[66] Mahabharata 3.311; spoken by King Yudhishthira
[67] Mahabharata 1.74; spoken by Queen Sakuntala
[68] Mahabharata 5.34; spoken by Mahatma Vidura
[69] Inspired by Mahabharata 5.36; spoken by Mahatma Vidura
[70] Mahabharata 1.90; spoken by King Yayati
[71] Mahabharata 5.42; spoken by Rishi Sanat-sujata
[72] Mahabharata 3.311; King Yudhishthira stating *'ahimsa paramo dharma'*, 'non-injury is the highest Dharma'
[73] Mahabharata 3.295; spoken by Savitri

[74] Mahabharata 5.28; spoken by King Yudhishthira
[75] Mahabharata 3.212; spoken by Rishi Markandeya
[76] Mahabharata 3.2; spoken by Saunaka
[77] Mahabharata 3.311; spoken by King Yudhishthira
[78] Mahabharata 3.2; spoken by Saunaka
[79] Mahabharata 3.215; spoken by Rishi Markandeya
[80] Details on each posture go beyond the scope intended for this book, though several books and websites on postures are available for those interested in learning more. It is recommended that postures be learned from qualified teachers and not from following books. As with any physical activity, if done incorrectly, these postures could lead to injuries.
[81] Mahabharata 3.3; King Yudhishthira practices pranayama
[82] Mahabharata 3.311; spoken by King Yudhishthira
[83] Mahabharata 3.270; spoken by Lord Shiva
[84] Mahabharata 6.19; spoken by Brahman
[85] Mahabharata 6.4; spoken by Minister Sanjaya
[86] Mahabharata 5.93; spoken by Lord Krishna
[87] Swami Vivekananda, *Karma-Yoga* 76 and 89.
[88] Mahabharata 5.33; spoken by Mahatma Vidura
[89] Inspired by Mahabharata 2.61; spoken by Mahatma Vidura
[90] Questions and answers derived from the section called 'Yaksha Prashna' in the Mahabharata 3.311. Lord Dharma asks questions and King Yudhishthira answers.

CPSIA information can be obtained at www.ICGtesting.com
Printed in the USA
BVOW011139230613

324067BV00016B/350/P

9 781482 053036